THE ORGANIC STIMULUS PLAN

SOLUTIONS THAT WILL TAKE AMERICA
FROM CRISIS TO PROSPERITY

BY ALEXANDER GROVER

FOR MY WIFE INDRE

FOR THOSE WHO STILL BELIEVE IN AMERICA

THE ORGANIC STIMULUS PLAN
SOLUTIONS THAT WILL TAKE AMERICA FROM CRISIS TO PROSPERITY

BY: ALEXANDER GROVER

COVER DESIGN BY: MEDIA MENU (ESTONIA)

ISBN: 1452801312
EAN-13: 9781452801315

BISAC: POLITICAL SCIENCE / ECONOMIC CONDITIONS

WEBSITE: THEORGANICSTIMULUSPLAN.COM
CONTACT: INFO@THEORGANICSTIMULUSPLAN.COM

"ETERNAL VIGILANCE IS THE PRICE OF LIBERTY"

- THOMAS JEFFERSON

This quote is inscribed on the guardian statue in front of the National Archives in Washington DC

"A DEMOCRATIC SOCIETY DEPENDS ON AN INFORMED AND EDUCATED CITIZENRY."

- THOMAS JEFFERSON

This quote is on the wall at the Mt. Prospect, Illinois Public Library

Preface

I spent most of my life doing what I thought I was supposed to do. I studied hard in high school and received a degree in Nuclear Engineering from Kansas State University in 1994. At the time, I had high hopes that leaders would realize that nuclear power was the key to our future. After graduation, I entered the "real world" and endured a long period of under-employment selling Nordic Tracks before joining Price Waterhouse and then, finally, the US Navy, where I became an Intelligence Officer. As cool as the title sounded, I was soon frustrated by the bureaucratic nature of the job and, after completing my obligation, opted to enter the private sector. I went to work for Ericsson in Sweden then later for Sears Holding Corp as a Six Sigma Project Manager. As my career advancement opportunities hit a ceiling, I decided to pursue my MBA in Marketing from the University of Illinois at Chicago. Later I would work with family and friends in a real estate investment trust and then for a European investment bank. During that time I married my wife Indre, and we returned to the United States to start a home-based cookie manufacturing business, which has given us firsthand experience in entrepreneurship.

I am still reeling from what is known as *reverse culture shock,* the adjustment associated with returning to America after living abroad for an extended period of time, whereas my wife is experiencing the culture shock associated with moving from Europe to America for the first time. Prior to returning, we were both excited and optimistic about living in America, the nation where "impossible is nothing" (Adidas slogan). America has always been a nation where leaders make decisions based on a grand-unified vision.

During my extended stay abroad, I have seen other parts of the world where people are catching up with America through innovation-- not only in technology and standards of living, but in their outlook on progress. They are realizing it is more profitable to cooperate with rivals and conduct business in a transparent, honest manner. In Brazil, I witnessed police officers refuse bribes and in India, tasks that used to take days, like opening a brokerage account, now take only an hour. Many times I have actually seen things being done more efficiently in other parts of the world. While Americans, for example, invented the Internet, E-trade, and PDFs (portable digital files) we still do banking with paper checks, while most people in Eastern Europe complete all their transactions electronically, a process which moves money in only 20 minutes.

When I went abroad, I saw that people can, in fact, dramatically change their old ways by sheer free will, just like our nation did in the past. While the U.S. remains one of the most capable countries, our elected officials continue to filibuster us into long term and gradual self-destruction. But no one is asking, "What happens when the stimulus runs out?" We are becoming more risk adverse; managers these days want to maintain existing processes, "flying below the radar as not to make waves" instead of leading by taking calculated risks, making necessary investments to reinvent the processes, to achieve greater long term output with less resources. We hear "think outside the box" but when you actually do it, you may stand-out, risking your career.

It seems we have lost our drive to be the best at everything; we are becoming second to Asia in technology and car manufacturing, we are winning fewer

Olympic gold medals, and we have not won a Miss Universe pageant since 1997. It is difficult for us to accept that we may have to look to other nations' innovations for inspiration, like adopting Europe's standardized GSM mobile phone infrastructure, offering a single infrastructure standard and frequency by which telecom operators work together to expand coverage area for all phones. Whereas in America, we have separate companies setting up separate networks on different frequencies and infrastructure, forcing us to change our handsets when we change operators

This book is for those Americans who are frustrated with our current politicians, who instead of making our future more optimistic seem to be doing the opposite. This book is for those who know something is wrong but can't figure out exactly what it is, those who find life is getting harder instead of easier, and those who want to achieve something meaningful but find themselves beaten down by office politics and red tape.

This book intertwines my own life experiences with economic data and factual references to reveal a simple truth: that while our destiny remains in our hands, we must invest our time into democracy to regain control of our lives.

This book is divided into four parts:

<u>Part I</u> is a self-introduction and an account of what I witnessed during my travels that pertain to the current economic situation and looming debt crisis.

<u>Part II</u> explains key issues that are affecting our society and economy.

<u>Part III</u> reveals how we the people can stimulate the economy. It outlines specific projects that will propel our country into a new era of innovation and prosperity based on economic fundamentals

<u>Part IV</u> offers resources and insights on how we can regain our culture of innovation and greatness.

THE ORGANIC STIMULUS PLAN

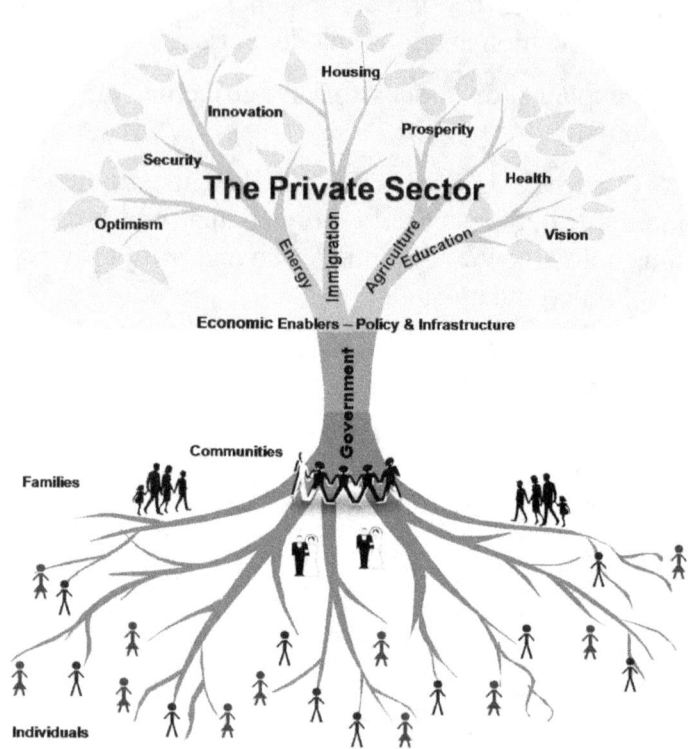

BEGINS WITH WE THE PEOPLE!

The Society Tree illustrates the relationship between individuals, communities and government. Our daily actions and decisions as a society in aggregate determine our future. It all begins with us!

CONTENTS:

PART I - BACKGROUND

Inspiration

"America is the only country that can do anything when it puts it mind to it." – A Danish traveler I met in the Copenhagen Airport en-route to Estonia (2005).

When I joined the ranks of the unemployed in early 2010, I decided to collect my thoughts and write a book that would hopefully get people to think differently about what has happened to us in the past decade, so that we can make this decade more prosperous. This book is a self-published and self-funded effort, offering my view on how we can put this country back on track to greatness.

In addition to sharing anecdotes and observations from my life, *The Organic Stimulus Plan* offers detailed solutions for repairing our current state of affairs, using both deductive reasoning and quantitative and qualitative data. These ideas are not a silver bullet, but, in the long term, they will make us stronger and more independent. To implement these solutions, we the people must move from passive to active, participatory citizenship. These solutions will lift our nation from its current anemic state, held together with Band-Aid solutions, to sustainable prosperity.

Everyone in government seems to be trying to assign the blame rather than fix the problem. It often seems that both Democratic and Republican leadership put trivialities in front of long-term national interest, spending too much money without a well-defined financial plan.

Our economic problems are not only rooted in the leadership's mismanagement of resources (especially time) and its lack of a unified long-term vision, but also in our apathy toward the voting process. Many people do not understand how current events impact our daily lives. Not only do we need to change our leadership, but we also need to activate our citizenship. We need to be planners and doers.

Additionally, mass media, whether it exhibits a liberal or conservative bias, makes money by bickering about our current state of affairs, not by offering real solutions to our problems. As long as there is debate and disagreement, these media shows will thrive; friction, after all, creates heat. Media does not make money when people agree to find a happy medium; instead, conflict is their fuel. By perpetuating discontent, they inflate their ratings and make their network more appealing to advertisers, thus leading to increased revenue.

The Age of Counter-Productivity:

During the past 10 years we have seen technology advance while our standard of living and quality of life have retreated in the opposite direction. Technological tools, however, should help us do a given job faster, thus increasing our productivity, which leads to an increased quality of life. For example, prior to the invention of nail guns, it used to take me a few hours to frame 2x4s for a shed. Now, however, I literally "staple" the 2x4s together, saving time and raising my "per hour" earnings. If I keep my work to eight hours per day, my pay increases without cutting into my family time, thus improving my standard of living and quality of life.

While we are now given the electronic tools to increase our productivity, we also find that goods are getting more expensive and our free time is on the decline. Cell phones appear to be as much a detractor as an enabler to get things done, ringing in the middle of conversations or causing distractions while driving. And users are finding that "better" operating systems like Windows Vista are only causing more problems.

	1998	2008	Change
Median Income (2008 Dollars)	$51,295	$50,303	-2%
Dollar vs. Euro (Hi-Low Average)	0.932	1.423	53%
Median Income in Euro terms	€55,038	€35,350	-36%
Average House Price	$181,900	$292,000	61%
State College Tuition/yr (2009 dollars)	$4,285	$6,585	54%
Operating System	NT 4.0	Vista	-
Global Mobile Phone Sales (million)	176	980	457%
Price of Gasoline/Gallon (2009 dollars)	$1.35	$3.23	139%

Sources: US Census Bureau, ECB, The College Board, Gartner Dataquest & DOE

Wages are not keeping pace with rising costs despite increased productivity and technological advancements

We are all supposed to be, nowadays, cross functional, inter-departmental and fully flexible. However, what managers fail to realize is that, over time, going broad comes at the expense of going deep; we are sacrificing the gaining of expertise in a specific area, needed to create meaningful innovation. Multi-tasking has not taken us anywhere in the past decade. Michael, a former college roommate of mine from Seoul, Korea, once told me, "When you chase two rabbits at once, you don't catch either one of them." Teamwork requires that everyone must do what he is good at; then a skilled project leader should bring it together as a finished product. But what we find these days is that everyone is doing everything, and the leader ends up micro-managing every task.

Time is the most misunderstood and mismanaged commodity. It is both limited and expiring. I always find myself saying, "Money comes and goes, but each day only happens once." In order to become good at something, we must invest time on a task. Time invested in one task comes at the expense of another. Moreover, we need time to rest and recharge so that we can keep building on our expertise. This go-go-go, always-connected mentality is burning out our society. We have not advanced by increased standard of living, increased wealth, or increased quality of life; in fact, it's been quite the opposite. The Dow Jones and NASDAQ indices have yet to recapture highs set over a decade ago.

Average wages are going down while consumer prices are going up. I remember growing up in St. Paul, Minnesota, when my dad, who was an engineer for 3M, was able to support a wife, afford the mortgage on a single-family home in a good neighborhood, purchase two cars and raise two kids, all on his one salary. Moreover, he still had money left to save and invest. Now it takes a double income just to buy a townhouse.

We need to ask the question, "How good are these tools in reality?" For all this hard work and increased productivity during the past 10 years, why is it harder now to maintain a basic standard of living than it was before? We are on a Japan-like trajectory, it seems, witnessing a drop in asset prices while wages stagnate or even decline. Japan, the world's third-largest economy, experienced three decades of rapid economic growth (10% in the 1960s, 5% in the 1970s, and 4% in the 1980s).[1] Japan was eventually able to establish itself as the world's second largest economy, but this growth came to an abrupt halt when both real estate and stock prices busted in the late 1980s. Since then it has not experienced any substantial economic growth.

The solution is perhaps counter-intuitive: we may need to start doing less to get more done.

Rolling Back Campaign Finance Restrictions

In January 2010, the US Supreme Court ruled 5-4 to lift the ban on political spending by corporations in candidate elections, ensuring that, in effect, corporations can fund political campaigns unfettered.

I feel we are already a media-driven society at the whim of large corporations. Pitchmen come into our living room and persuade us to buy all sorts of gadgets, schools broadcast commercials that promise prosperity after two years of study and food companies bombard us with pitches to eat increasing amounts of processed food.

We are a society on autopilot. We go through our daily routines of commuting, working, grabbing lunch if we can and then working more. By the time we get home, we want to enjoy what is left of the day by relaxing with our family in front of the TV, where we are exposed to hundreds of corporate messages. When vacation time comes around, we are either too broke or too tired to go

---

[1] Japan, Patterns of Development, www.country-data.com

off to some far off land and truly relax. Instead, we take a packaged trip and remain bombarded with advertisements and messages to buy more trips, package upgrades and add-ons.

Because of changes in campaign finance law, now corporations will be able to run commercials against candidates who threaten their bottom line, provided they put a disclaimer on the advertisement. Americans in either political party should be deeply concerned about the coming age of corporate oligarchs. The effect of this decision is that large corporations will start to influence local elections, giving them immediate returns on their investment.

For example, a big-box retailer may desire a site that is out of their reach due to current zoning. The site may be a park or even a property of historical significance. The corporation will then start running ads in favor of a politician who in turn will enact legislation that will secure or even seize the land and turn it over to the corporation for development. Corporations can also get local officials to enact laws hindering the entry of possible competitors, like local small businesses.

There is a tire shop around the corner from me which always offers good deals, much cheaper than any chain. Hypothetically, City officials elected on behalf of a consortium of large corporations could pass zoning ordinances that make it too costly for this tire shop to stay in business at their current location. In an extreme scenario, corporations could even get elected politicians to overturn environmental regulations, such as the ones that removed DDT and lead from our food and homes. Then they could air commercials that would convince us that the removal of these regulations would reduce taxes and create jobs. If you think this isn't possible, remember that we have already witnessed auto companies fighting fuel efficiency standards.[2] Additionally, imagine what would happen if McDonald's and Coca-Cola started funding the election of local and state officials. In turn, these officials would then have the incentive to authorize the purchase of these foods for school lunches.

If we are not vigilant, we could vote ourselves into a Soviet-style system where a relatively small group of CEOs gain monopolistic control over their given sectors. Our landscape will be littered with big-box stores and fast food joints and, over time, our consumer choices will dwindle while prices start to rise. As time passes, politicians will be installed at all levels to ensure that the legal system protects corporate interests. We will compete for mundane jobs at Target or Wal-Mart. Opening a new business would only be for the social elite. Not only will we lose opportunity, competition and choice, but the innovations that result from open free-market competition will be lost as well.

The Point:

Don't believe everything you see in the mass media. The broadcaster's business model is driven by advertising. And the leaders you might believe in are mostly funded by wealthy donors or special interest groups. Although the people who represent these special interest groups have the same voting power as we do, they contribute

---

[2] John M. Broder And Peter Baker, Obama's Order Is Likely to Tighten Auto Standards, *The New York Times, January 25, 2009.*

substantially more to campaign funding than we do. This may explain why simple yet sensible ideas that would benefit the masses rarely get passed.

With all the bias in the media, we have to do our own research and draw our own conclusions. Fortunately, the raw and un-manipulated statistical data is readily available on government websites, including the Census Bureau, Bureau of Labor and Statistics, Department of Agriculture and Centers for Disease Control. It requires effort to get this information and put it into a form in which you can interpret it. However, doing so will help you make better decisions and become an active citizen. We can win our lives and our nation back from the brink if we, as individuals, begin to participate in our democracy.

The Role of Government

We live in an era where people either want a total welfare state or complete anarchy. There are many ongoing debates over what government is supposed to do and not do. Ultimately, our government needs to look out for the best interests of the common American.

This concept of government acting in the parental role is nothing new. It extends back to pre-historic times when a council of tribal elders carried out the responsibility for overseeing judicial matters. In essence, they possessed legislative powers. They would hold forums and take decisions on strategic matters such as what crops to plant, whom to have treaties with and how much food to store for winter. They outlined a long-term strategic vision and detailed the associated actions needed to make it happen, while the younger members of the tribe concentrated on day-to-day work, such as hunting, gathering and raising children.

However, sometimes it seems that politicians exploit our business in that when we do not take the time to be properly informed, all kinds of laws can be passed. Case in point: Congress automatically receives pay raises every year while the rest of us see our salaries remaining stagnant or declining. Although Congress voted not to get a raise in 2010, the average congressman still made $174,000 in 2009.The irony is that Congress has to vote against getting a raise. If they don't vote, they automatically get it.[3]

When Middle America thrives, so does the rest of the nation. The poor can advance into the middle or wealthy classes, and the rich grow their own net-worth through increased sales, business expansion, investment and innovation. In 1999, when the economy was rocking and rolling, Bill Gates net worth touched $101B whereas in 2009 it was around $50B.[4] Push the middle, and everyone wins.

Level Playing Field

The government's role first is to create policy that allows general society to thrive in a sustainable manner. To do this, they must ensure that everyone has equal opportunity. This concept is not to be confused with advocating equal pay for unequal jobs or lowering standards of excellence for minorities. Everyone who is qualified should be able to compete in the marketplace unhindered. The government must ensure that people who have accumulated massive resources and wealth cannot unfairly stifle competition with such practices as dumping (selling their items below cost for the sole purpose of putting competitors out of business), collusion and manipulating local officials to their advantage.

We are living in an age in which regular Americans are receiving pink slips and pay cuts while Wall Street

---

[3] Brian Montopoli, Congress Keeps Automatic Pay Raises, *CBS News Politics* March 13, 2009.

[4] Forbes 400 Wealthiest List 1999, 2009

Bankers and Fortune 50 CEOs are receiving bonuses for failure and massive severance packages after quitting or getting fired. In essence, they get a golden parachute while the rest of us get a golden shower. Executives at AIG, for example, have complained about having to take pay cuts after having put the U.S. economy at risk with irresponsible derivatives trading and still receiving $182 billion in taxpayer money to stay afloat. In the end, Anastasia Kelley, AIG's General Counsel, received $2.8M in severance for quitting her job over her objections to a government imposed pay cap of $500,000 per year.[5] Suzanne Folsom, AIG's former chief compliance officer received an estimated $1M in severance after resigning in protest to the $500,000 per year pay cap.[6] Where do I apply for such openings?

Moreover, investor Warren Buffet's tax rate was 17.7% in 2006, while his secretary's tax rate was 32.9%.[7] Warren Buffet challenged other Fortune 400 CEOs by offering them $1M if they could prove that they paid a higher percentage of taxes than their secretaries; no one called him. I find it surprising that extreme conservatives are complaining about illegal immigrants not paying taxes on their extremely low wages, while the top 1% of this country is paying a much lower tax rate than the average

---

[5] Steve Eder, AIG's Anastasia Kelly to get about $2.8 million in severance, *Reuters*, Dec 30, 2009

[6] Andrew Hard, $2.8M, $3.8M, or 'Several'—How Much Is AIG's Departing GC Going to Get?, *Corporate Counsel*, January 5, 2010

[7] Alex Crippen, Warren Buffett and NBC's Tom Brokaw: The Complete Interview, *CNBC*, October 31, 2007

worker. Moreover, many in this elite group have off-shored billions of dollars to evade the IRS.[8]

There is a valid point that uncollected tax revenue from illegal immigrants adds up to about $10B per year.[9] However, they do spend much of what they earn in the local economy to pay expenses such as rent, food and fuel, thus supporting American businesses. The National Restaurant Association and Associated Builders and Contractors argue that our economy would be worse off without illegal immigrants, who fill many jobs in the food services and building sectors.[10] From a financial perspective, it would be more fruitful, in terms of cash recovered, if we pursued the elite who knowingly evade taxes.

We never hear the extreme right condemning about the 52,000 Americans who set up Swiss bank accounts to hide a total of $14.1B from the IRS as of 2009.[11] This money is sitting offshore, earning interest and making no contribution to the U.S. economy. I find it ironic that extreme conservative Americans, most of whom earn 1/319th of what their CEOs receive, can fight so hard for elites who don't even know them.

---

[8] Pat Norton, The End of Swiss Bank Secrecy, American Institute for Economic Research, December 23, 2009

[9] Keyonna Summers, Illegal Aliens' Not Paying Fair Share Of Taxes, Study Says The Washington Times, June 6, 2006.

[10] Krissah Williams, Labor Groups, Business Seek Immigration Law Overhaul, *The Washington Post*, January 20, 2007

[11] Mark Scott, UBS on Trial, The End of Secret Banking? *Businessweek*, July 10, 2009

Average CEO to Worker Pay Ratio

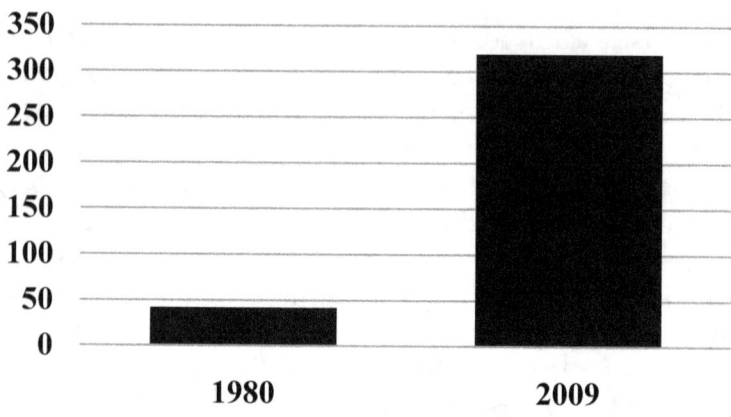

Source: Institute for Policy Studies - United for a Fair Economy

CEO pay has accelerated but what about our pay? After all, companies are profitable because of their workers. Is this where all of our routine unpaid overtime ends up?

One argument for the wealthy having to pay a lower tax rate is that they create jobs and build the economy; this is a valid argument. There should be rewards for the risks and sacrifices they made. I personally know many wealthy people who lost their family and health in the process of building their businesses. Many of them struggled financially for many years to get their business running. However, they should still have to pay their fair share of taxes because they are using more of the nation's infrastructure and resources to their benefit. Moreover, even after paying these taxes, they will still be far wealthier than the middle class.

14

Enabling Innovation

The government must ensure there is adequate competition so innovation can occur. Spurring innovation is an all-American tradition going back to colonial days. America has always been the world leader in patents and Nobel prizes. For generations, the U.S. government has supported research and development, private industry, and education. As a result, great advances like the space program, computer and data processing technology, nuclear power, and the Internet have been developed.

Laws such as the Sherman Anti-Trust Act which limits cartels and monopolies and Eminent Domain are needed if the system or a community starts to stagnate. Eminent Domain is a necessary yet controversial government power needed to help our nation's economy grow. The power has always existed in the United States, through the 5th Amendment and, to a lesser extent, the 3rd Amendment. Eminent domain is defined as the inherent power of the state to seize a citizen's private property, expropriate property, or seize a citizen's rights in property with due monetary compensation, but without the owner's consent. The property is taken either for government use or by delegation to third parties who will devote it to public or civic use or, in some cases, economic development. The most common uses of property taken by eminent domain are for public utilities, highways, and railroads; however, they may also be taken for reasons of public safety.[12] Without eminent domain, much of the

---

[12] Wikipedia: Eminent domain

infrastructure that benefits the masses would have been sacrificed.

In life, there are neither easy nor absolute "everyone wins" solutions when strategic decisions are at stake. There have been and always will be times when the needs of the masses far outweigh the needs of individual entities. We have to bear in mind that we live in a nation, and we benefit from its infrastructure. Roads, schools, defense, and even sewer lines were paid for by taxpayers long ago. We as citizens need to be willing to sacrifice our homes when the need is justified, provided we do receive proper compensation. For example, people living in Virginia Beach near the Oceana Naval Air Station received more than their land was worth when the U.S. Navy purchased their land for military housing. [13]

However, we must be watchful that eminent domain is never used for private re-development. This is, however, sometimes a grey area. If a prime piece of land would, if redeveloped, yield more jobs and raise the value of the property around it, then the government is justified in purchasing this land for a business. The business must, however, ensure that the homeowners are duly compensated, with the right to present her own valuation

In India, there is very little government involvement. Everyone earns and pays in cash, making taxes almost nonexistent, but there are also few paved roads, meaning people must walk to get their water. Moreover, security is a big issue. Poorer Indians often must sleep on their cash

---

[13] Deirdre Fernandes, Beach Initiative at Oceana yields new homes, less density, The Virginian Pilot January 25, 2010

to prevent theft. This is why societies and hierarchies form over time, even in anarchist states. People group together and specialize, trading their output for something that they can't produce on their own.

Smurfs are a great example of division of labor and specialization: Greedy Smurf makes cakes which he exchanges for home services from Handy Smurf. Both Smurfs are able to gain more by trading with each other than making everything themselves. Depth of skill allows one to increase the value of his output enough to trade for something of higher value.

Vision

Our nation needs long-term vision and leadership with a stepwise plan on how to achieve it. We need leaders that will clearly outline our choices and give us the benefits and consequences of each. We accomplished such big goals in the past with Manifest Density, putting a man on the moon and building the Panama Canal. Today, however, it is difficult for many individuals to see beyond next year, let alone the next 20. However, if proposals are explained with the realistic benefits and sacrifices needed, there would likely be mass support. Instead, legislators try to sneak pork through in the form of riders on bills.

Long-term planning creates a sense of certainty for the future. Today, many people earn good wages but suffer from stress and anxiety due to uncertainties about what lies ahead. This frustration impacts a well-known indicator called consumer sentiment, which wreaks havoc in the financial markets and ultimately the working person's 401K. Government, like parents, should guide us to a brighter future – offering something to look forward

17

to and something to work toward. They must ensure their promises will be delivered.

We must move beyond great speeches to decisive action if we are going to get back on track to reach the projected $35 trillion economy by 2050.[14]

Defense

Finally, the most important role of government is to provide national defense against enemies foreign and domestic. The government through taxation takes up a collection from the public to raise an army, train troops and buy weapons. Military spending is an expense. Much like spending on insurance, we pay the premiums but hope that we never have to use the policy. Besides the construction of ships, aircraft and submarine, military spending also goes to vocational education and leadership training roles through programs like the GI Bill and ROTC.

However, the fact remains that the more we spend on security, the less we can invest in the infrastructure that enables domestic growth and creates jobs. Spending on security must be done wisely, as security jobs do not create a significant number of other jobs. If we were to spend money to build a bridge between two cities, for example, not only are a number of construction jobs created, but over the long term there will be jobs created by the increased commerce resulting from the two cities being connected. If we spent money to buy a few 737s to

---

[14] Dominic Wilson & Roopa Purushothaman, Global Economics Paper No: 99, *Goldman Sachs*, October 1, 2003

help United Airlines service some isolated reaches of our nation, the return would be greater for the overall economy than if we bought F-35s fighter planes. Throughout history we have seen that societies that build an economy around the military don't thrive: Sparta, the USSR, and North Korea are prime examples.

Defense spending must be planned in a calculated and deliberate manner to address the real threats that exist to our wellbeing and economy. One visible return on military spending is the use of a Navy to keep shipping lanes open by combating pirates on the high seas.

Government is Inevitable

While watching wildlife specials, we come to realize that even animals have some sort of government. Lions, organized in prides, divide duties by taking turns hunting or raising young. The female lions do the actual hunting while the male lions protect the kill. Orcas, or Killer Whales, are organized in pods which also have hierarchies in place to ensure the calves are protected and there is food to eat. If government were to be completely eradicated, over time people will begin to form similar "tribes", deferring authority to elders or an alpha-male. In essence, government is natural, part of our DNA.

No matter where we go there will always be a need for some form of government to help manage limited resources and harness the collective power of the people. Instead of eliminating government, we the people must manage it. At the end of the day, we are the government.

Despite its faults, the US Government is the most efficient large-nation government in existence. Federal government services continue to innovate by offering online services to improve efficiency while streamlining payrolls and saving time. The states too, are run quite well. In Virginia, I can file my company's tax receipts online and the money is automatically drawn from my bank account.

However, we can still do better. The average federal worker's pay is about $71,000 annually, whereas the average private sector worker makes $40,000 per year. Moreover, the number of federal workers making $100,000 or more went from 14-percent to 19-percent during the first 18 months of the recession, whereas more than seven million Americans in the private sector lost their jobs.[15] Moreover, federal workers get unbelievable benefits such as paid health insurance and 20 business days of vacation per year. What this means is that eventually young brilliant people will be more motivated to enter the public sector, which will do little to help our economy grow. Ultimately, we need entrepreneurs.

Government will never be as efficient as a corporation, because their role is to give us basic services which are merely enablers for the greater economy. The post office does not make a profit, for example, but the companies using the post office do. However, if the same re-engineering methodologies that were applied to make America's corporations more competitive back in the 1980s and 1990s were applied to government agencies today; it would vastly reduce waste and redundant processes. Aligning all government metrics so that every government process has measurable output in terms of

---

[15] Jack Cafferty, Federal workers make twice as much as private sector workers, *CNN Politics*, Dec 14, 2009

direct impact to taxpayers (the customer) will give rise to new opportunities to merge and consolidate functions while improving service.

Government positions should be a place for young graduates or mid-career workers to get training or experience before entering or returning to the private sector. These jobs should be competitive, challenging and rewarding. The fixes won't be perfect at first but will instill a culture of continuous improvement into the government, which will not only help us get more with less but will also make the bureaucrats' work more meaningful.

In some levels of government there is a need for people with special skills, such as NASA scientists. These positions must be identified and compared with equivalent positions in the private sector. Employment offers should be made accordingly. People who enjoy their work tend to stay for the job satisfaction more than the pay.

Although we are in the age of instant information, in which it is easy to find out how much the government spends, nothing will change unless we the people act. In addition to showing up to vote with our ballots, we also need to vote with our dollars. Any big change begins with a small shift in attitude within each of us.

Autobiography

I am not a famous author or well-known literary thinker. My views are not aligned with a specific political party. Most of what I believe is based on logic, facts and data and my analytical perspective is usually financially-grounded. Money is a limited resource that symbolizes stored time and work, and I believe it is important that we set priorities and make decisions that consider this. That sometimes means giving up one thing for another. I believe:

- Neither Democrats nor Republicans address my concerns in their entirety. I feel that Greens, Libertarians and Tea Party activists can be too emotional, not grasping the modern day realities of inevitable globalization and modern economics in pragmatic terms.

- Optimism is a wonderful medicine. A strong, stable economy can cure a large number of social ills.

- Nuclear power is currently the only viable large scale power generation solution that will satisfy our energy needs. It is not perfect, but with proper management, it will eventually win support from those opposing it.

- While we need a strong military, the invasion of Iraq based on the "imminent threat" premise and the misguided notion of expeditionary nation building (at the expense of our own people) is quite troubling to me. We need fewer subs and jets and more body armor and Mine Resistant Ambush Protected (MRAP) vehicles.

- I am against gun control but am for background checks. There should only be lists of people who are not allowed to own guns, instead of a list of those who are.

- I am against outright handouts without conditions but am for education, child support and community outreach and development programs that assist people in a constructive manner during difficult times.

- Our health care system is a mess, but I am not sure the current plan in its chopped-up state will be effective, unless a series of preventative health-care measures are also implemented.

- The presidential debates are superficial; they only test the candidates' ability to improvise and come up with memorable one-liners. The debates are more of an audition for talk show host than for political office. Instead, we need *detailed presidential presentations* with substance, which would help voters make better decisions. We should give each candidate two to three hours to deliver a detailed plan on national TV that addresses the country's pressing problems, and a plan and budget on how to solve them.

Origins

I was born in St. Paul, Minnesota, while President Richard Nixon was in office. My parents had emigrated from India after my father received a scholarship to study engineering at the University of Minnesota. When my father, who worked for 3M, was transferred, our family moved to Prairie du Chien (PDC), Wisconsin, a beautiful town situated where the Mississippi and Wisconsin Rivers meet. Growing up, my greatest concern was how to remain true to the Minnesota Vikings while living among all those Green Bay Packer fans. I started 5th grade at BA Kennedy Middle School, where I first began to develop a sense of business and political awareness, learning about the Dow Jones Industrial Average and the Camp David Accords where Jimmy Carter facilitated the peace accord between Menachem Begin of Israel and Anwar Sadat of Egypt.

After watching *Red-Dawn*, a 1983 movie about the USSR invading the U.S., my junior high classmates and I got together and discussed contingency plans for PDC: hiding out in the hills and hunting deer to get by. We spent hours hiking in the woods after school looking for hideouts; we rode bikes across town and climbed 50-foot trees without any safety equipment. We were not the bubble wrapped children of today[16] – that's for sure. I remember how we PDC kids used to put up major resistance when it was time to go inside.

Suburban Chicago

Later, my Dad was transferred by 3M to Chicago. I finished out my Jr. High School in Bolingbrook, Illinois, at BJ Ward Middle School. This was a culture shock of a different sort. I went from a school where I was one of the only non-whites to a school where I was one of the only non-blacks or non-Latinos. I remember offending just about everyone on my first day. One kid told me that my black and gold Nike sneakers indicated Vice Lord gang

---

[16] Elizabeth Donovan, The Bubble Wrap Generation of Kids, *Time Magazine*, November 20, 2009

membership, while another kid told me that my hickish plaid shirt meant an allegiance to the Latin Kings.

The environmental change was frightening; essentially I had gone from rural Wisconsin to a suburban satellite of the inner city. This is when I began to bury myself in books.

Eventually, because of my father's commute, we moved to Downers Grove, Illinois, where I started my freshman year at South High School. I wanted so badly to redefine my life that I went out for the wrestling team. Looking back, I should have tried out for soccer and swimming instead. However, the greatest lesson I learned from wrestling was that if you show up to every practice and take your lumps, not only will you get into exceptional physical condition, but you will be ready to face adversity in real life.

Although I barely won any matches, the lessons in perseverance learned from Coach Krupke lasted a lifetime. I studied hard to get into a good college. Downers Grove South was a very competitive high school, with first generation kids whose parents had come from all over the world -- Poland, Lithuania, Thailand, China, Vietnam, India and Pakistan. They were all aspiring to be doctors, engineers and lawyers. Because we lived near Argonne National Lab, a particle accelerator, many kids were also aspiring to be scientists. South High School, I would later find out, was more difficult than most colleges in the U.S.. In my senior year, I decided that I wanted to be a military officer and went through the West Point application process. I was turned down due to eyesight problems. Heartbroken, I accepted a scholarship to the University of Southern California instead.

Rowing Crew

At USC I got into rowing eights, which meant getting up very early in the morning to move a 60-foot-long, 2-foot-wide shell gracefully through the water. Rowers eat all the time to keep from starving to death; I was burning so many calories I could barely keep my weight above 150 pounds. I barely got by at USC, as the demands of engineering, physics, calculus and chemistry were difficult to meet while also training in a sport. Also, the financial pressures were immense. While I was able to pass with respectable grades, it was not enough to keep the scholarship.

At the San Diego Crew Classic, I met some rowers from Kansas State. Being from the Midwest, I knew where Kansas was but never imagined myself living there. It was such an interesting concept, rowing in Kansas. Prior to leaving LA, I remember waking up one morning and watching the LA Marathon from my apartment window. I went downstairs to my friend Chris's apartment, and we made a pact that one day we would run this race together, no matter how much it hurt.

In the fall of 1990, I enrolled at Kansas State University and joined the crew team. K-State had a unique Nuclear Engineering curriculum. I was intrigued by the idea that nuclear power was be the most viable energy alternative to fossil fuels, and the key to America's energy independence. Luckily, most members of the crew team were engineering majors, so I had a great support system and a team full of potential tutors. In my senior year, I was finally able to pull my GPA over 3.0, and was eligible to apply for graduate studies. In my senior year, I also would fly back to LA to run the Los Angeles

Marathon with my friend Chris. After graduation, I began a job as a computer programmer at Price Waterhouse (PW).

Life is a Journey not a Destination

PW was intense. My first day lasted until 9 p.m. I was living with my parents in Downers Grove, Illinois, and having to commute by Metra and car for over an hour each way. It dawned on me quickly that being corralled in a cubicle and chained to a computer writing code at age 23 was not for me. I was too young for this kind of job. During the dead of winter, I started talking to a Navy recruiter and within a few months, I was headed for Officer Candidate School (OCS). What ultimately convinced me were the pictures of beautiful red-brick condos on the beach; this, the recruiter said, was where the officers live.

I showed up at Pensacola Naval Air Station in the summer of 1995. The Candidate Officers started to yell at me: "Place your feet at a 45-degree angle, back straight, thousand-yard stare!" Shoelaces had to be tied over, then under, in a symmetrical fashion. There was so much chaos that I had to try not to laugh out of nervousness. One candidate officer came up to me and said "Grover, you want to bust up, don't you?" But as I started to say "No sir!" I just lost it. OCS was not as physically demanding as I thought it would be. If you could run 1.5 miles and do 67 push-ups and 100 sit-ups, you were fine. However, it was mentally and emotionally demanding, since I was completely unfamiliar with Navy customs. The prior enlisted men were the best at coping with all the inspections and mind-games. My strengths, however, were academics and physical fitness, although I had the additional problem of being rhythmically challenged. Marching out of step, I always seemed to be half a second off, which angered Gunny Krank. Consequently, I was given massive punishments in the form of push-ups and forced to roll around with my rifle in the sandpit. I also had to write 500-word essays one letter at a time using a stencil, known as a "timewaster."

By graduation, I was in incredible shape, and I was still smiling. If it were not for the lessons in endurance from Coach Krupke in high school wrestling, I never would have made it through OCS. To this date, I consider my wrestling coach and drill instructor one of the best life teachers I ever had.

After graduation and a brief tenure at nuclear power school, I was assigned to U.S. Special Operations Command as an intelligence officer. This job was perfectly suited to my interests in geopolitical affairs. I also attended Army Airborne School, where I learned how to fall from 1,200 feet. While the Army seemed to have more fun than the Navy, I would never have traded in my Navy uniform for the green; the Navy tradition and the love of the various uniforms were ingrained into my psyche. My Navy career ended in Virginia Beach, at the U.S. Navy Marine Corp Intel Training Command (NMITC), where I learned IT/web technology. The late 90s were an exceptional time to be a job seeker, and eventually I decided to leave the Navy and pursue the private sector.

Midsummer

Since college, I had this dream of living abroad in Sweden or Finland. While in college I used to read in admiration about the culture and history of the highly organized Nordic countries. My first overseas position was as an engineer with Ericsson Business Consulting Services in Stockholm, Sweden (Ericsson is one of the largest companies in Sweden and one of the world's largest communications technology companies along with Nokia and Motorola). I assisted in the development of specifications and concepts for wireless applications on mobile phones. Sweden was a really cool place with lots of beautiful girls, great technology and excellent public transportation. People were very friendly once you got to know them, and the friendships were real and genuine.

Bar33, also known as Wap2Bar, was my claim to fame in this small world. It was a drink and cocktail dictionary that could be retrieved by Wireless Area Protocol (WAP) for which I designed the specifications, database architecture and pseudo-code for this product, then handed it off to Joakim and Magnus, my Swedish colleagues who coded this application using SQL, ASP and WML. The coolest part about the program was that specific names could be inserted into the drink recipes. For example, instead of just saying vodka, it could say *Absolut* Vodka if the company paid for the spot. For the most part, the experience in Sweden was dreamlike; however, the high levels of taxation made it difficult to get ahead. After a certain amount of time, I wanted to live in something bigger than an apartment in Husby, an outermost suburb of Stockholm.

My colleagues and I would spend weekends heading to Tallinn, Estonia, by ferry. Upon arrival, Estonia looks like one of those planets visited by Captain Kirk and the Star Trek crew. A surreal, dreamlike medieval landscape,

Tallinn's old town is a castle fortress dating back to the 15th century. Inside this fortress are vast numbers of Estonian girls, known for their incredible beauty. It was almost difficult to believe that a place like Estonia actually existed.

Satisfaction Guaranteed <u>or Your Money Back</u>

One evening I received an email from Scott, an old high school friend in Chicago, who told me I had an in-demand skill set--wireless experience and Microsoft certification—and that he was going to help me get a job. A month later, I interviewed for a position as a wireless consultant at Sears Roebuck and Company. This was my first encounter with making really good money as an hourly consultant. My job was to help integrate outside software and hardware into the new Sears Smart Tool Box, a laptop that would increase the efficiency of Sears Product Repair Service technicians in their servicing of customer calls. However, I was also getting razzed by regular Sears's employees on a constant basis about being a highly paid outsider.

Eventually I interviewed for a salary position at Sears as a Six Sigma Blackbelt (Project Manager). The major theme of Six Sigma is being able to define a process so that it can be measured in numerical terms. During the interviews, I met Curt, a West Point graduate who was just getting out of the Army. He was from Minnesota, and we hit it off as friends. We liked to go to Accent Café, a Polish nightclub in Mt. Prospect that was frequented by mostly Eastern European immigrants, and to The Living Room in Schaumburg, a bar frequented mostly by cougars. Curt, however, soon met the girl he later married, which put an abrupt end to our antics. Our second day of training for Six Sigma was September 11, 2001.

My coworkers and I rushed to watch the monitors in the lobby then saw the second plane crash. I remember thinking that the only way for us regular day jobbers to beat "the enemy" was to keep working hard. I devoted myself to Six Sigma, learning how to make SIPOC (Supplier-Input-Process-Output-Customer) charts which maps a process from supplier to customer. We were tasked with reducing warranty abuse coverage which, in broad terms, was defined as getting Sears out of paying for stuff under warranty that was damaged by use beyond the warranty guidelines. Sears had this iconic policy of "Satisfaction Guaranteed or Your Money Back" that has been around for over a century. The interpretation of this policy is highly subjective. The most difficult part of this project was how to quantify the size and magnitude of the problem - taking descriptive words and turning them into something solid that could be measured quantifiably.

We narrowed the scope down to lawn and garden, for example, and, within this segment, the tractor mowers. Now we had to figure out how big this problem was. We did so by retrieving various samples containing around 1,000 service records each. This would assure the stakeholders that our findings would be statistically sound. We were able to discern if the warranty work was valid by not only reading the technician comments but also by seeing how many times Sears PRS technicians visited the same customer within a two-year time period. We read such comments as "customer uses equipment for landscaping business", "third time visiting in one month to replace blades" and, the most interesting, "tractor mower found at the bottom of a swimming pool". There was even a customer who had a DUI and was driving his Sears riding lawn mower like a car. Every time it would break down, Sears would go out and fix it. More amazing than these comments was that the fact that the incidents were serviced under the warranty at no cost to the customer. The mower that was found under the pool was hoisted out and replaced at no cost! The Sears service technicians, along with the tech managers and even the district managers, would sanction the repair of these obvious cases of abuse and overuse out of fear that the customer would call Sears HQ and their branch or region would be reprimanded with a NCR (National Customer Relations) Complaint. I failed to understand the seriousness of such a simple complaint, but no matter what the outcome, the regional office was charged $450 for each call. Any sensible person would think that NCR would set limits on warranty coverage, but this was not the case. Their job was to prevent the marketing phenomenon in which a really angry customer tells twenty others about their experience. Sears aimed to prevent this by giving the customer whatever he asked for. We used to hear from district and regional managers, "It's a matter of how loud and high the customer can shout." Some skilled customers had figured out the code and they would call key executives in headquarters, getting not only their problems solved but also receiving some perks as well.

As a Six Sigma Blackbelt, I was already making waves by informing the stakeholders (key leaders who were involved in the process) that we would be studying this problem more closely. I was still a bit naïve, being relatively fresh out of the Navy and Sweden, to think that corporate managers with University of Chicago credentials would be thinking how to fix their company at the strategic level. Instead, many of the key managers feared that their P&L (Profit and Loss Statement) would take a hit when we stop covering commercial usage under warranty and customer complaints increased. Sears offered a bonus structure in which a manager could receive up to 230% of his salary as an additional payout, based on his P&L at year's end. This meant managers didn't want to make waves.

As we started to explore the root causes of this problem, we concluded that we could not stop all warranty abuse; however, we did spot regular commercial usage; essentially, 20% of our cases accounting for 80% of the money spent by Sears on warranty abuse coverage. We knew we couldn't entirely eliminate this problem. But if we could reduce it by 25%-50%, it would save substantial amounts of money down the line. There was a catch, however: these commercial use customers were also Sears's biggest spenders, buying multiple pieces of equipment on a regular basis. This problem had to be handled carefully.

In the end, we found that there were two places where we could fix this problem. The first part of our solution included changing the scripts at the inbound call center where service calls were answered. Instead of just setting appointments, the call center representative would also probe the customer for the causes of the problem. The second and less successful part of our solution was to have the technicians refuse service on extreme cases while assuring the field managers that the company would stand behind the local branch and the service technicians if he customer were to call corporate and complain.

However, it was easier to intercept the customers at the call center. The CCN (Customer Care Network) representative would simply ask, "Are you using this tractor for commercial use?" Amazingly enough, many customers would answer yes and even tell us how well their business was doing because Sears did all their maintenance for free. In these cases, the call center representatives would calmly inform the customer of the warranty limitations regarding commercial use, and offer them their money back for the warranty (about $135 compared to the $450 average spent on each warranty abuse coverage case). Hence, the "or Your Money Back" part was cheaper for. Although our solution was far from perfect, the Director of Finance for Sears Product Repair Services affirmed our savings at $2.5M for the year.

Eventually I was given a second and more complicated project, adjusting the parts pricing model. Essentially, pricing inefficiencies were costing the company money. I approached this task with the same dedication I had with the warranty abuse issue, offering solutions that ultimately increased Sears' revenue by $7M. But instead of getting a bonus, I was given the option to continue working with a pay cut or to be laid off. Apparently, in the course of pushing for results, I upset some decision makers along the way. Later I would find out that some of these managers were involved in an accounting scandal to show inflated results, boosting their bonus payouts. If I knew that I was being measured by skills in office politics rather than returning money to the company, I would have played a different game. At this point I decided I better take advantage of my veteran's benefits before they expired. As a veteran from Illinois, I was entitled to three years of free education at any of the state-funded institutions. I was not going to pass up a free education that would put me on a more rewarding career path.

Liatuad MBA at the University of Illinois at Chicago

The University of Illinois at Chicago (UIC) offers outstanding programs in medicine, business, engineering and IT. I was excited to go back to school after many years in the workforce. In the first year of my MBA program, I studied the basics of marketing, finance, accounting, statistics and management. Although these courses were interesting, I was a bit surprised how much memorization was involved in graduate work. Exams seemed to come at the expense of more debates and discussions. I could not understand how people would pay over $600 per credit hour (in-state) per class for this knowledge; I was extremely grateful that my GI Bill and the Illinois Veteran's Grant were taking care of the expenses and incidentals. Ultimately, I learned that MBA programs are more of networking opportunities than learning opportunities. The classes were topical, meaning we were expected to pick up most of the relevant knowledge in our respective careers. Eventually, I decided to have a bit of fun. When we were tasked in our courses to visit and study a company, my classmates chose consulting firms, law firms and factories; I chose Hooters. I contacted their regional director and spoke to her about doing my practical work at one of their locations. Shocked at first, she assigned me to a Hooters restaurant in Buffalo Grove, Illinois. I met Greg, the manager, who introduced me to the staff. In the course of my study there, I found that Hooters was a serious business that had above-industry-average growth rates. I ended up writing several papers, entitled "Sex Sells, and It's Legal", about this company. I was impressed by how innovative the chain was in terms of management and marketing. During my studies, I also worked as a bookkeeper in the Electrical Engineering department and as an ESL (English as a Second Language) teacher. In the class, the students learned enough English to write short letters and stories. ESL allowed me to see that the undocumented people living in our society are ultimately nice people, with great senses of humor, who ultimately just want to work. The summer before my graduation, I enrolled in the "Doing Business in Brazil Program" in Sao Paulo, Brazil. I lived with a family near the school who spoiled me with great food and warm hospitality. We spent eight hours each day in class went on field trips and visited government economists. On the weekends I went with my host family or classmates to cities like Uba-Tuba and Rio de Janeiro.

For our final presentation for the program, my classmates and I researched Gol Brazilian Airlines, the Southwest Airlines of Brazil. During the course of this study, I learned that Brazil is not only an agricultural powerhouse but an industrial one as well, producing aircraft, appliances and machinery.

Return to Estonia

After completing my MBA, I found that society had entered the age of certifications. To advance, one must obtain a CFA to perform financial analysis, a PMP to manage projects, a MSCE to click a mouse and plug wires into a hub, and so on. There are now certified resume writers and career coaches. Preparation for these certification tests has become an industry in itself. "Pump and dump" learning has become the norm: cram, take an exam, then forget most of what you learned within a week. I often wonder how the distraction created by these certifications affects our real productivity in the workplace. Moreover, I wondered what had happened to the idea of gaining experience through actual work and the mentorship of senior leaders.

In part due to this understanding and my exhaustion from my studies, I took my savings and returned to the magical place I had always enjoyed while living in Sweden. When I arrived, there was a boom underway in Estonia. The economy, especially the housing sector, was roaring. Estonia had invested in IT and telecommunications infrastructure that allowed cell phone coverage throughout the country, free Wi-Fi access in all the cities and villages, and paperless banking that enabled Estonians to send and receive money from mobile phones. In fact, no one I knew in Estonia ever used a paper check. Although this was an emerging economy, the public and financial sectors were already more efficient than those in the West. Rob, an old friend from Sweden, hooked me up with a good deal on a flat. Amazingly, I managed to get a mortgage for this flat with just a U.S. Passport and web print-outs of my U.S. bank statements. Eventually I would live back and forth between Estonia and Virginia Beach, flipping real estate and importing trucks.

Along the way, I made the acquaintance of a former Goldman Sachs investment banker. We talked about the unrealized potential of the United States. I was convinced that investors were so caught up in emerging markets that they forgot that the U.S. was still a long-term growth story.[17] I put together a convincing presentation on how the Virginia Beach Oceanfront area would make an ideal investment for a strategic investor focused on long term real estate and currency plays. This former banker liked my presentation so much that he offered me an excellent position in his company.

Joakim was a very charismatic Swede-Finn who knew how to get things done while still remaining compassionate. Bosses like him are rare in America. I was more productive in this position than in any other I had had, enthusiastically working lots of overtime. However, Joakim made sure his workers were also taking time off to "recharge our batteries." The corporate away-days had a lot of athletic events to break up the monotony of the long, drawn-out financial presentations.

My colleagues were an interesting group of highly intelligent people from all over northern Europe. We would go out to parties and nightclubs and go horseback riding and even snow sledding. Visitors, especially American ones, would mistake our company for a modeling agency. Our reception staff, legal department and accountants were all the usual Estonian girls, making them supermodels by American standards. There were three economic analysts in particular who aroused the senses on a daily basis. Lelde, Mariana and Monica always arrived at work together, walking down the hallway in formation, one in front and two behind. They had confident strides and beautiful smiles. They weren't

---

[17] Goldman Sachs Report 99

just pretty faces, however; these girls would research relatively unknown small companies in emerging markets, then create summary reports for the investment committee to review. Working with these "economic models" was a great pleasure. They were warm-hearted, highly educated girls who could talk about globalization and macro-trends in Asia.

Tallinn's expatriate community was interesting, to put it mildly. It was made up mostly of Scots, Brits, Irish, Americans, Aussies, Kiwi's, Italians, Germans, Swedes, Icelanders and Finns. We often converged for parties, which were several orders of magnitude wilder than anything you see on South Padre Island. These parties were all ages, all nationalities, all beliefs and all inclusive. Estonia was in essence high school revisited. My flat used to be the epicenter of such events. It was funny that I didn't drink, but I still had a full liquor cabinet. In Estonia, it is customary for guests to bring alcohol, and I would always end up with more drinks than I started with. Thus, I would have to start another party to finish the surplus from the previous party…

During my travels and escapades, which were becoming routine, I met the girl who would later become my wife, while checking in for a flight at the Vilnius airport. She flew to Tallinn with her friend for our first date. One my American friends joined us, and we made a pretty good weekend out of the event. Three months later we were engaged in Chicago on top of the John Hancock tower, and soon after we married at the Bellagio in Las Vegas.

Meanwhile, I worked very successfully as the director of marketing at the Estonian investment bank. This position not only fit my knowledge, skills and aptitudes, but was also fully aligned with my interests and personality. Moreover, Joakim's family-like corporate culture made long hours feel purposeful and rewarding. In the end, however, I had to leave this job to secure my wife's green card to the U.S.As required by immigration; we had to return to America within six months.

I was concerned when I left Estonia that it was entering a severe recession. I collected my thoughts in a book called *The New Estonian Golden Age* which offered long–term, economically-viable solutions for Estonia's crisis. It was a choppy book in areas, written during evenings and on weekends, and it was refused by Estonian publishers because it mentioned reconciliation with Russia. However, the book eventually rose to #1 in the Estonia category on Amazon. I find it amazing that the book is still receiving Estonian orders to be printed in the U.S. and shipped back to Estonia at tremendous cost.

Later, I would get a call from the Estonian Development Fund to speak about the book. To my surprise, the seminar was attended by a number of prominent politicians, fund managers, bankers and business leaders. I gave a brief overview and shared some of my philosophical beliefs, which included the idea that Estonia has to try to retain the best attributes of its culture while still embracing change. I emphasized that Estonia should focus on one of its key strengths—candy. Kalev makes excellent chocolate and marzipans which they could manufacture abroad. However, what seminar attendees found most interesting was my talk on Medical Tourism—how to make Estonia a bridge between Indian doctors and American patients.

Re-Immigrating to America

After leaving Estonia, I decided to defer my job search and start a cookie manufacturing company with my wife and mother. For a long time I had been baking extra large whole grain cookies packed with nuts and Ghirardelli chocolate chips. Everyone asked me to bring my specialty cookies to parties and office events. I even gave one to my wife on our first date, which obviously made a lasting impression. While I was working in Estonia, I started to finalize a few recipes and write a business and operations plan for the business. When we returned to America, I spent the first 2-3 months renovating the kitchen to meet the Virginia Department of Agriculture and Human Services standards for home-based food manufacturing companies. Meeting health regulations was difficult but not impossible. I had to write an operations manual, make sure the kitchen met all the building codes and also create food labels. Once this was complete, I was granted the right to operate out of my kitchen, and we started to bake and sell the cookies under the name *Squirrel's Bakery*.

We now market our products online, in the local farmers' market, at festivals and at independent grocery stores. During the course of selling our goods, my wife and I met some interesting people. We once accepted an invitation to a woman's house, which turned out to be a Multi-Level Marketing (MLMs) pitch for Mona Vie, a $40-per-bottle Acai fruit drink. At the woman's house, we listened to a pitch delivered by a former baseball player who extolled how Mona Vie cured his ailments and made his marriage better. He also showed us his online bank statements, which confirmed that he was making $15,000 per week selling the drink.

There are two misconceptions about MLMs, one from critics and one from supporters:

First, critics believe that the products are scams. I generally have found that the products are quite good and in some instances worth the money. For example, my wife and I use Herbal Life and Juice Plus for our vitamin supplements. I speculate that the reason these products are sold through MLMs is that they are too expensive to sell in a high-volume retail environment where shelf space is scarce.

Second, supporters of MLMs give you the impression that you will make money selling their products without actually having to work. But while one can indeed make money in MLMs, like any other business, you must be willing to invest a great deal of cash and time.

My wife and I continued to work very hard to market our goods. We ran some ads, but the sales were just not enough to earn a living. Although several banks were willing to give us a business loan, they required that we use our house as collateral. Eventually, I decided to look for a job to help support our baking business through its start-up phase.

Government Contracting

I contacted a Junior Military Officer (JMO) recruiting firm that matches candidates who have military leadership experience with a variety of companies. They lined up an interview for me with for an engineering consulting firm with immediate openings for travelling management consultants. The pay was entry level, and the job required a great deal of travel and long hours. I had the first interview with Huey, a Senior Operations Chief who would not look me in the eye. All I could see was the top of his bald head while he told me about the position. However, the session went pretty well and I had a second interview over the phone the following day with Steve, another Senior Chief Operations Officer. Just as the phone interview started, however, F-18s screeched overhead. Steve asked me who had interviewed me prior, and my mind just went blank. It took me over a minute to recall Huey's name, starting the interview off on the wrong foot. He spent a great deal of time telling me about the amount of travel and low pay, and I responded that I was looking for career development more than pay: the standard party line BS that one tells interviewers in a tough job market. Eventually I told him I needed to go, and needless to say, I did not end up working for that company.

I feel that job interviews today are ultimately ineffective; all that is being tested is the applicant's ability to play "the interview game", rather than his true skills and motivations.

Perhaps this lack of depth and willingness from management to learn about potential employees explains the growing lack of passion in the American workplace in the last decade. The best actors, not the best people, are getting hired. The Conference board states that Americans hate their jobs more than ever before; with less than 50% saying they're satisfied.[18] From this experience, I learned how to fake enthusiasm for a lousy job the same way that actors pretend to be fantasy movie characters.

Two weeks after snubbing Steve, I responded to an ad in the classifieds for a RFP/RFQ (Request for Proposal/Quote) Proposal Writer position at a local engineering company. I had no idea what a RFP/RFQ proposal writer was, but I wrote a compelling cover letter that landed me an interview. This was an 8a firm (woman- or minority-owned company) which meant they were able to compete in a smaller pool for select government contracts.

This company specialized in providing systems implementation, training and maintenance to the U.S. Department of Homeland Security. At the interview, Dianna, the owner of the company, and Jeb, the president of the firm, told me about the Department of Homeland Security, their firm, proposal writing and contracting. Jeb was a retired Navy Captain whose speaking skills were quite disappointing. He never spoke in definitive terms, just in vague parables. In the end, the job sounded easy enough – just learn the government format and write away. I hoped that I would be able to keep this job until something better came along. They offered $45K per

---

[18] Live Science Staff, Americans Hate Their Jobs More Than Ever, *Live Science*, February 26, 2007.

year, which when adjusted for inflation was lower than my pay in the Navy 15 years earlier. However, I needed to support my home business, and something was better than nothing.

Looking optimistically at this new opportunity, I did some research on RFP proposal writers. It turns out there is an entire subset of specialized employees dedicated to writing proposals to get government contracts. Once you are efficient at this, the job can pay upwards of $100K per year. Experienced writers charge upwards of $100/hr. This seemed exciting in theory: if I dedicating myself to learning a new skill, after a few years I would be able to make a decent living.

On the first day of work, I sat in on a meeting where employees were arguing over grammar on a draft proposal. I was then taken to my cubicle, an instrument created by corporations to dehumanize workers and force their psyche into compliance. I immediately felt insignificant. Soon my greatest pleasures would be going to the bathroom and eating lunch. I ignored these feelings, realizing that I would just need to write proposals until something better came along.

I was introduced to the staff, which was nothing like Trigon Capital or anywhere else for that matter. Moreover, everyone was very subdued, almost tranquil. They all seemed afraid to talk about anything more than lunch and the weather.

The only interesting person in the company was the IT specialist, Dwight. He looked like Will Smith: he was 46 years old but looked 26. Ironically, he already had grandkids! He was outgoing and believed in taking walks after meals. He brought in a pull-up bar which we secured over the door to stay fit. We had many interesting conversations about data simulation and modeling, the use of Second Life to simulate ergonomics and medical coding outsourcing. However, it's almost impossible to start-up a business to take advantage of such opportunities while working full-time jobs and going through the rigors of everyday life.

Jeb told me to learn my job under JJ, an older independent consultant in his mid 60s who appeared to be a victim of bad portfolio management. He was angry at the company for not listening to his advice regarding proposal development, at his asset manager for losing his retirement savings and at the fact that he could therefore not retire. Is this what I had to look forward to in life? He was probably an honest, hardworking man who had followed all the "rules", but ended up with a bag of circus peanuts just before retirement.

I was told that I had three months to become fully proficient at RFP Proposal Writing. I started to read the Shipley Book, the bible of proposal writing. It was my only reference point. When I would start referencing the book at meetings, the proposal manager Shelly would shoot me down. She was an older, hostile woman, probably in JJ's situation, whose whole life was a series of three-ring binders and Microsoft Word documents. She could only offer criticism. Meanwhile, Diana was breathing down my neck. I needed to learn faster. Eventually, to appease her, I applied the roles of a game I learned at Sears: let the others know what you are doing and that you're actually busy, even if you're not.

I began writing past performances, examples of similar work done in the past. I noticed that the examples of RFQs and RFPs were quite superficial when describing what the company actually did. There were comments such as, "Twenty guys showed up and did data entry." It did not describe in detail what the data was, how complicated was the task, how this task was essential, or how these tasks were connected to the greater organization. I really wanted to rewrite these documents from a financial or Six Sigma perspectives to show proper resource management, efficiency and value creation. However, my approach was denied. I was told these were service jobs; we just needed to put bodies in seats. My argument in return was that I had once had a cleaning lady who was able to make measurable improvements in her job performance by leaving her chemicals at the house under the sink. By eliminating her usual setup time carrying the chemicals inside every week, she saved me $60.

I was surfing the net during working hours looking for a better job, I realized that I did not want to waste my life in a cubicle, and I spent my extra time instead creating an outline for this book whenever time permitted.

When the holiday season arrived, we were told that we would have to work over Christmas. That Friday we had the company Christmas party, which would also be my wife's first American corporate party. She was nervous about her attire and dressed nicely. When we arrived, she noticed that all the women except Dianne, the owner of the company, were dressed somewhat sloppily.

I explained that in America, people become their jobs and everything else is second: good-looks, kids, family, and exercise – basically everything worth living for. People get wrapped up in consumerism, taking on huge amounts of debt to buy plasma TVs, cars, clothes and so-on, to the point where they end up imprisoning themselves in a job they really don't enjoy but have to keep just to cover the payments. Meanwhile, we sat next to Jeb, the company president, and his wife. My wife and I both forgot to read "How to Act at the Company Christmas Party" on Yahoo Jobs, namely the part about not disagreeing with the boss or his wife, not even respectfully.

The boss's wife was telling us how she was pursuing a Masters Degree online without having to conduct extensive research, teach undergrads or provide a vigorous defense of her thesis. She told us that her classes were in Second Life, an online virtual 3-D interactive world. On a similar note, something not mentioned on career advice websites, if your wife is young and hot and the boss's wife is old and fat, you're supposed to either not bring your wife or feed her Twinkies the months leading up to the event. This wife jealousy thing can really wrangle with your American career.

I told her the reality was that Second Life is an escape for those who are lonely or left out of society. It offers them a place to interact and activate senses that are dead in their real world. My wife thought what I said was logical, but the boss's wife seemed offended.

Eventually the food arrived and we moved on to more mild discussions. At corporate functions, you're supposed to talk but not say anything. This is even truer in the South. I asked questions about the age of her kids and where they went to school for the rest of the evening and this seemed to repair this little scuffle we had Second

Life. I sure missed the days in Northern Europe when I was the only sober person at corporate functions, calmly witnessing scandalous after-hours antics that would rival any college frat party.

Although I don't think there really exists a better way to solicit and respond to RFPs, it's a painful process which at best could be streamlined by doing the process online like USAJobs.gov. But this may only offer marginal time savings, as every RFP is different and requires experts to review them. However, this raises the question of why we should pay government contractors almost twice and even three times as much as what the government pays its full time employees who many consider already overpaid. Some may argue that these are only temporary contracts that only a professional services firm can do. However, the government has temporary hiring provisions in place like those with TSA or USAID. The Transportation Safety Authority and US Agency for International Development are able to hire and fire employees in the same manner as the private sector or on an as needed basis for the duration of the contract, whereas the rest of the Federal Government has to go through an extensive process to reduce excess or redundant workforce.

As I found out more about the inner workings of government contracting, it became quite hard to believe in this job as a long-term endeavor. History has shown that bubbles inflate, then burst unexpectedly. Now we're in a government spending bubble, paying 2-3 times more than needed for a given service. This trend cannot last any long. Since the field of RFP writing only has guidelines and not rules, I decided that I would write in quantifiable terms how doing business with our firm would yield savings down the line equal to or greater than what they were paying us. This approach required me to talk to the actual people in the field. In order to do this, I had to get past Marci, the human resources specialist.

I explained to her that I wanted to talk to our employees in the field and ask them if they could send me a few resume bullets that quantified their work in terms of improved efficiency or dollars saved. Most of their resumes made them sound like overpaid data entry clerks, and I was worried that this might make us less competitive in the long run. Marci, however, denied my request, and eventually I got my way by impressing the boss with buzz-words.

Dianna was a chronic micro-manager. She was constantly asking me if "I was really there." In order to look like "I was there," I kept printing out pictures of my wife and putting them on my desk, but she had already caught on that I was thinking of different employment.

Eventually, I was called into Marci's office, where Dianna sitting in a chair. She told me that she had bad news. I could only feel relief that the misery was going to be over. I was glad that I was able to make it through the holidays and at least make a little money to keep afloat and pay down debt. But now the realities of life had to be faced once again.

21st Century Job Interviews

Resuming the full-time job search in these dire times is frustrating. It is a 6 a.m. to 9 p.m. endeavor. The first step is to write a resume that shows a company that you can add value and are mature and stable. Since my work history was varied and frequent, I hired a resume writer from Ladders.com, and for $600, she wrote me a stunning resume.

One must apply to every job individually. You must convince the hiring manager on the other end that this is your dream job and all your past experiences coincide beautifully with the challenges of the job. Applying for job after job, I found myself getting into a tiresome routine of telling the same story 20,000 different ways. Some applications, especially the ones for those six-figure government jobs, can take the better part of a day, as you have to answer questions and fashion your cover letter accordingly. Later a friend of mine told me that most of those government jobs are already spoken for and are only posted as a formality. They have already planned to hire someone they know. Although I have the highly desirable skill set of Marketing Manager, the only interviews I received from online applications were for local companies who advertised on Linked-in or in the *Virginian-Pilot* newspaper. In addition to applying online, I sought the help of recruiters, mostly the ones who aid former military officers. There were a few phone interviews, one of which was with Dow Chemical. Eventually, however I was told by the recruiter that this position had been filled internally. Recruiters are an excellent source for jobs because they have direct contact with the hiring manager. So in a sense they contribute to the hiring decisions of companies.

During the job search process you inevitably end up talking to a lot of different people: other interviewees, recruiters, hiring managers and even random strangers. It seems like there is an inordinate number of boring people out there. I always like to talk about the cookie business, world travels, and writing, but talk of the weather or the NFL bores me. The phrase that annoys me the most when I try to share some of my creative endeavors with other people is, "You seem like you have too much time on your hands." I think that we all have a lot of time on our hands. It's what you do with all this free time that defines your life. Some people choose to spend their time watching sports, while others invest their time in hobbies that are constructive and enjoyable, but not profitable. And then there are those who invest their free time into building a business. But in reality, while you may give up "the boss" when you own your own business, you replace him with demanding customers. Still, I am taking the path described in the book *Rich Dad Poor Dad* by Robert Kiyosaki: use the job as a means to fund a business. My free time, little by little, is used to build an entity that will set me free from corporate bondage. This plan has to be kept secret, but at the same time I wanted to put the bakery on my resume. After all, I spent the past nine months dressing up like a squirrel and selling cookies while gaining valuable skills in process management, marketing, branding, food labeling and statistical quality control.

After about a week of sending resumes and making phone calls, I started to receive a few calls from recruiters. One recruiter told me about a position at a well known financial advisory firm. I had often considered the idea of becoming a financial advisor to help people realize their dreams by helping them better manage their lives. But the reality is that I would be lucky to set-up a portfolio investment plan that would outperform a monkey over the long term.[19] I went through their long and involved process to learn about the training program and the firm.

It all begins with a lengthy process of phone interviews and questionnaires. When I finally met a financial advisor at one of the local branch offices, I was well aware of the rigors of the job: door-to-door sales, phone call follow-ups and lots of rejection in a highly saturated field. The focus of the business model is to get assets under management or everyday people's money invested into fund products as to which they collect a fixed percentage of instead of aiming for absolute performance and taking only a success-based fee.

Henry, the financial advisor, told me the worst part about the job was watching his clients lose money, which I completely agreed with. However, this conversation took a turn for the bizarre. He started telling me how he racked up debts, lived above his means and lost control of his finances. I asked him how he felt about the future of this country after it had racked up debt without a clear investment plan or exit strategy. He assured me that it is all temporary. To me, Henry looked like he was trying to

---

[19] Paul B Farrell, Chimp '99 champ! Makes monkey of Wall Street, Marketwatch.com, Dec 30, 1999

convince himself that Santa-Claus was going to come down the chimney and make it all better.

I have spoken to many financial advisors over the years, and what I find is that very few of them know anything about the effect of global macroeconomics on the long-term health of individual portfolios. Most advisors are mere salesmen, not economists or stock-pickers. They rely on the home office to do this and they sell what the computer tells them is a good fit for the client's needs, like bonds and mutual funds. I suppose that a car salesman doesn't have to be a mechanic to sell automobiles, but I think it would be wise to consult a mechanic to see which cars are the best cars.

My Mom invested in funds with this same firm, which I was applying to, and all her "safe" index tracking funds have been stuck in neutral or lost money during the past five years. Her self-selected portfolio of Krugerrands and Indian fixed deposits did much better. Despite her losses, however, her financial advisor sent her a fancy printout showing how the funds "outperformed" the selected benchmark. One thing I learned from being in the financial industry is that the word *"outperform"* does not always mean *makes money*. The term simply means it did better than a benchmark to which it was compared. Thus, if the Dow Jones Industrial Average goes down by 30% and the fund goes down by 20%, you outperformed! But what most investors want is *absolute return*. I would find it difficult as well to tell a granny that after her 401K got nuked that she still outperformed. Investors need to understand that the higher the potential gain, the more likely you will lose a lot of money--the layman's definition of risk.

I believe that most people would be better off developing their own portfolios, investing in them accordingly and taking measured profits along the way. ETF (Exchange Traded Funds) investments are approaching $1 trillion, as they offer low fees and are highly liquid.[20] I suppose that in reality there will always be a need for such salesmen. However, I believe that the industry is in dire need of performance-based versus fee-based funds and investments. Investment advisors always argue that they cannot predict the future, but I argue that it is their job to help forecast and prepare us for the incoming weather. The truth is that all of the financial crashes had precipitating indicators foretelling the calamities to come. I believe, for example, that too much good news is a warning. For example, this long period of low interest rates will not only cause erosion in the value of the dollar but also start precipitating a hyper-inflation time bomb or even worse, bring about a period deflation.

Giving the best financial advice is usually not profitable for an intermediary such as a financial advisor. Case in point: during my MBA studies, I took Accounting 500 with Professor Brian Leventhal, who emphasized the idea that "Cash is king, always." At the University of Illinois, I also learned about the "Rule of 72" which means that 72 divided by a given interest rate will give you the doubling time. For example, 72 divided by my mortgage rate of 6% means that I will pay double for my house in 12 years, or 72 divided by my 8% savings rate in India means my

---

[20] Matt Turner, ETF assets to pass $1 trillion, *Bulletin Wealth*, November 6, 2008

money will double in 9 years. Let's say I have a credit card with 20% interest. According to the "Rule of 72", in a little over 3 years, I would have paid twice my balance in interest. Hence, compounding interest can work for you or against you. I wish that I learned the Rule of 72 earlier; if so, my life would have been vastly different today.

I recently spoke with a mortgage broker friend about the possibility of paying off my house early. He advised me that it was a bad idea; instead, he said, take out more equity and invest the cash. The lesson I learned from this encounter was that it's a bad idea to ask a guy who makes a living by lending money about paying off debt.

My belief is fiscally conservative; I believe that paying off my house not only brings peace of mind but also increased cash flow. Economics, in principle, is the collision between mathematics and human emotions. Nobel prizes are dispensed to those who can model human behavior as it relates to consumption, also known as behavioral economics. There is a great sense of relief and a change in one's state of mind when one is free from debt. Freedom from debt surely has an effect on mathematically-based economic indicators, such as consumer confidence. Peace of mind is highly underestimated by the banking industry because it's difficult to quantify.

Most mortgages compounded over 30 years amount to 2-3x the initial loan amount, which in my case amounted to $168K over the principal. Moreover, the interest saved over the remainder of the loan, which in my case was $147,000 over the next 19 years, was almost as much as the initial purchase price of my home of $153,000. Although I owned the house for over ten years, my payments went mostly towards interest. In the later years of the loan, the payments would start applying significantly towards principle. This is how amortization works – the banks get paid first, then you.

My friend's (the mortgage banker) counter-argument was that I could invest the same amount of money into stocks and beat my mortgage interest rate of 5.75%. However, he failed to mention the associated risk and uncertainty of "hedging against the mortgage rate". Recent history has shown that funds and other financial instruments can be quite unpredictable. Moreover, we are entering an age of grave uncertainty with new variables such as globalization, political unrest and resource scarcity. Staying up all night worrying over investments and house debt not only has an effect on one's health, but I am sure it ripples into the economy.

I could use any increased cash flow to improve my standard of living, making only my minimum monthly payments and purchasing more cool stuff. But paying off a house makes you "self-insured." The equity in the house acts as your life insurance policy, so you don't have to pay monthly premiums. It is my belief that if more people owned their property outright, we may all reach our goals of financial freedom sooner. This can only be achieved by taking deliberate measures to pay off the principle balance early, just after a home purchase, which usually means putting off other purchases such as new cars and exotic trips. For example:

- I have forgone the purchase of a new car and associated expenses, allowing me to pay down my mortgage at a rate of $800 per month for five years, amounting to $48,000.

- Since I returned to America, I have given up using a cell phone, which is saving me at least $40 per month. My belief is that if a cell phone is so important, any company I work for will pay for it. Applying this money to my mortgage, I will pay down $2,400 in 5 years.

- I have started to brown-bag my lunches, which is saving me $6 per business day, allowing me to pay down $7200 in 5 years.

In addition to the above advanced payments, there are compounding effects at 5.75% per annum from not having to pay the associated interest with the additional paid-off principal. After years of attacking my mortgage principal, I refinanced what little was left to a much lower payment, increasing monthly cash flow and quality of life in a truly organic manner – having real cash in my pocket instead of having to use more credit.

I also gleaned from Professor Leventhal's advice that it's always a good idea to keep cash on hand. The best investments are made during periods of distress which arise unexpectedly (i.e. high quality pre-foreclosure homes or stocks trading below book value just after a major market correction). The winners of these investments are usually the quickest ones to respond and capitalize on the limited opportunity.

"It is not the strongest of the species that survives, nor the most intelligent that survives. It is the one that is the most adaptable to change." - Charles Darwin.

If I knew better back then, I would have forgone every discretionary expense during my first five years working to pay off or save up for a house, minimizing the long term interest pay-out. If the pressure of bills is reduced, workers will spend more time on exercise, with family, or pursuing hobbies. Moreover, when skilled workers exercise their power and demand more free time, it will open up jobs for more young college graduates. Companies will have to invest in young graduates, anticipating a higher turnover of their employees.

Currently companies are able to keep older workers who have lost their pension funds and must delay retirement; they therefore have little incentive to bring new people on board. This is good short-term business, keeping labor costs contained on the P&L (Profit-Loss statement), but in the long run, it hampers innovation. Also, companies which do not pipeline have to deal with the consequences of employees leaving for health reasons on short notice.

There used to be a commercial which conveyed the idea that managing wealth is even more difficult than accumulating it. What amazes me is that the accumulated wealth will do as much or even more to impact our lives than the jobs we pursue in order to gain this wealth. Perhaps our nation would be more financially stable if the average person learned a little about investments and economics, in the same way they learn the features of their new cars or iPhones.

When individuals take control of their lives, more wealth is spread among the masses, instead of ending up in the hands of a few elite Wall Street fund managers. These managers see the numbers, rather than the individual behind the pension plan. They need to be reminded that those numbers on a screen are the accumulated life savings of real people who are close to retirement.

Chris, a recruiter from another JMO firm, arranged an interview for me with a major pharmaceutical firm for a sales rep position. Prior to the interview, I had two rehearsal interviews with another recruiter from the same firm. He drilled me with questions like:

"Why are you interested in sales?"

"What are the characteristics of a good sales rep?"

"What are your Characteristics?"

"Sell me a tennis racket."

The key was to answer consistently when the same question was asked in various different ways. The key to the selling of the tennis racket was to probe the customer for his likes and dislikes about his current racket and his budget. I drove to Richmond in the middle of a snow storm to interview with Chuck, the district manager.

Chuck made small talk at first, but I knew this was a test in itself, testing my overall demeanor and affability. When we discussed my resume, I had to, as usual, explain where Estonia was and what I did while I was there. He asked the typical question: "What are you most proud of in your professional history?" I answered with a story about how I was able to link up my former firm with a major financial institution within the first few weeks of starting work.

During the course of the interview, Chuck was emphasizing how important it is to be likeable more than knowledgeable. He explained that one of the greatest challenges to becoming a pharmaceutical sales rep was the ability to get around the "gate-keeper," the one who keeps the doctor's schedule. I was under the impression that doctors are professionals who want to keep current on new and upcoming medications, techniques and practices. I did not realize the difficulties involved in getting five minutes to make an elevator speech. Chuck stressed the most important thing was to close the sale and get the doctor to write prescriptions. He told me that while the good reps get around the gate keeper, the bad reps have relationships but no closing skills. We had to push sales. He explained that we would be spending a good portion of the day driving from one doctor's office to another.

I believe that pharmaceuticals are an important part of medicine and doctors should be more willing to learn what's available in their specialty. There had to be a better and less expensive way, I thought, of relaying information from the drug manufacturer to the doctors. It seemed ironic to me that a doctor's receipt of factual information about a drug depended more on the salesperson's personality than what he actually knows about the product. Moreover, the costs of these inefficiencies inevitably get passed to the American consumer. We ultimately pay for the drug reps' cars, expense accounts (used to buy lunches for doctors), phones and laptops, along with their salary and commissions. I wonder whether people have died needlessly because the salesman was tied up at the receptionist's desk. We will never know.

Although we have this highly inefficient system of well-paid prescription drug pushers, whose greatest challenge is to charm the gate keeper, we also have the world's highest obesity rate and rising rates of depression[21]. We supposedly have the best medical care system in the world.[22] I came to the realization that the pharmaceutical industry depends on people's remaining sick. The industry needs doctors to write prescriptions rather than advise patients on the basics of eating right, exercising, and getting proper rest. I suppose that these companies would not be in business if they could not aggressively promote their products in the highly competitive marketplace among so many similar products. It is also ironic that they would go out of business if people made simple re-adjustments to their lives by investing in themselves.

This is the reality of our for-profit medical system, and it will be hard to fix. However, I believe there exists a better way for doctors to receive information about drugs, in which companies would not have to invest in a sales force whose value lies in sociability rather than knowledge ability. Navy pilots go through rigorous training, and yet they still have to take continuing education on a routine basis to maintain their qualifications. Perhaps doctors could be required to attend seminars during which all these drug companies present their products. This certainly would reduce costs while increasing quality of care.

---

[21] Reuters, Use of antidepressant drugs in U.S. rising fast, NY *Daily News.com*, August 3, 2009

[22] Robin Herman, Most Republicans Think the U.S. Health Care System is the Best in the World. Democrats Disagree, *Harvard School of Public Health*, March 20, 2008

About six weeks after leaving my government contractor job, I landed a public sector job as a Research Analyst at a regional economic development organization. Ironically, the same presentation about the investment potential of Virginia Beach that had landed me the job at Trigon Capital in Estonia, also landed me this job.

Virginia Beach

Virginia Beach (VB) is the largest city in Virginia and the 42nd largest city in America, with an estimated population of 440,415 in 2008. Its median household income in 2007 was \$61,234[23]. The majority of the city's economy comes from the U.S. Navy and from tourism. The city belongs to a region called Hampton Roads, "America's First Region" consisting of seventeen cities and localities. Unlike the five boroughs of New York, united under one city administration and mayor, each locality or city within the region has its own government, police department, mayor and website. The region's decentralized organizational style, however, has prevented the Hampton Roads area from developing unified public transit and major sports franchises.

I was transferred to Virginia Beach while I was in the Navy, although my dream was to return to Florida. I ended up buying a house and settling in. Our oceanfront with its three mile long boardwalk, according the Guinness Book of World Records, is considered the longest pleasure beach in the world. While long board surfing one day, I ended up catching the best wave of my life, and it was then that I decided I wanted to live here. In 1998, Virginia Beach was very affordable, with tremendous upside potential. I was partying with some scandalous people and befriended Angie, a realtor who landed me a house in Shadowlawn, a neighborhood adjacent to the oceanfront boardwalk. It was my ideal home: a red brick, two story colonial, four blocks to the

---

[23] Wikipedia: Virginia Beach

ocean, for only $150,000. Through my friend Bobby, I realized one of the greatest benefits of being in the Navy: the VA Loan! I was able to finance my first home without any down payment. The mortgage was huge at the time, but I already had a plan to rent out the extra bedrooms. I put an ad in the paper and rented the upstairs to Andrew, an engineer from the shipyard who was going through a divorce. These were good times for me. I was in the Navy, partying like a rock-star, and getting most of my mortgage paid for by a roommate. I also got a boost in my tax refund from the mortgage interest deduction. I left for Sweden after my initial commitment with the Navy was up to pursue an interesting opportunity in wireless technology at Ericsson Business Consulting.

Beach Property Investing

When I returned in 2005, I found my house in shambles, due to a string of bad renters and apathetic property managers. However, the house was worth far more than I paid for it. People were knocking on the door offering me $350K and up. I decided to renovate the house and make it my absolute home base. I also decided to pursue a real estate license so that I could save money on commissions when I purchased investment properties.

Obtaining a real estate license is quite easy. I downloaded a course from the internet and passed the exam with a near perfect score in 30 days. There is some math, but most of the course and exam covers ethics and contractual matters. After passing the exam and receiving my license, I joined my property manager's firm. I learned quickly that real estate prices are a function of what the property collects in rent. Thus, when looking at a property, it is very important to gauge its rental potential first, then look at it as a purchase. A rule of thumb I picked up along the way was never to pay more than 150x one month's rent for a given property, and to sell it when the value of the property exceeded 200x one month's market rent.

Virginia Beach is pretty much the same today as it was then, in that our city still lacks a visionary master plan for the oceanfront. Our beach and boardwalk are easily among the most beautiful in the world; tragically, however, this national treasure is being grossly under-utilized. The tourism season in Virginia Beach lasts from May to September, with Memorial Day and Labor Day being the busiest weekends. As an owner of a vacation rental property, I have personally lived through the boom and bust of summer and winter rentals. I would much prefer steady year-round business. There are a lot of nice places along the oceanfront with beach charm, but the "dive bars" and run-down eateries prohibit property values from being as high as they could be.

The owners of these bars and restaurants claim that they cater mostly to professional and business clientele making $60K+ per year, but the quality of their establishments seem to contradict this statement. Ultimately, these places end up attracting rowdy young college-age kids that deter the targeted professionals from entering. I always dreamed of our Oceanfront becoming like Rodeo Drive or 5th Avenue, with high class shops, boutiques, five star hotels and posh restaurants. Locals argue that our town doesn't attract that kind of clientele, but I am sure that "if we "build it, they will come." When the Ukrainians built up Yalta, the high rollers showed up. What we have is rare, and instead it has become a Mecca for drunks and drifters. Our tourist economy has much room for improvement, which could translate into lower taxes for residents.

Sleepy Town with Great Expectations

Our local economy is very similar to that of the USSR or North Korea in that we are mostly dependent on the military-industrial complex for our existence. Although the Navy creates jobs, it also limits growth. There are areas along the oceanfront where building heights are restricted because of low-flying jets, perhaps hampering our overall economic growth potential. Moreover, it is considered bad etiquette to complain about the noise created by F-18s roaring overhead, causing long-term hearing loss and maybe even stunting early childhood development.[24] The locals call it the "Sounds of Freedom"; I call it the sounds of imported fuel being burned right over my head. Freedom comes from having a strong and independent economy, which in turn funds the military.

When I was a U.S. Naval officer, I had the understanding that we were employed by the American people to protect the nation. Part of protecting the nation is protecting its economy, which means the military must yield to public interests, especially ones that grow the economy. In principle, the military is a security expenditure which must be analyzed against potential capital investment when the need arises.

---

[24] Babisch W, Kamp I, Exposure-response relationship of the association between aircraft noise and the risk of hypertension, *US National Institute of Health*, Jul-Sep, 2009

The Naval Air Station Oceana has been located in Virginia Beach since 1943. We have had this ongoing game of chicken with the Navy ever since. Oceana Naval Air Station is home to all of the east coast F-18 Hornets Squadrons. While the city needs the military to maintain its economy, the city council has allowed developers to build commercial and residential housing projects that encroach upon the Navy's flight paths and crash zones. Over the years, there have been numerous exchanges between the Navy and city on this issue. The Navy would decide it was time to move the jets, and then the city would come back with plans to limit building in these zones. Things cool down for a while and then a few years later, we rediscover that the encroachment problem has returned, and the Navy starts with another BRAC (Base Realignment and Closure) commission.

It is true that the Navy was "here first" and that they do create jobs. However, instead of using this "stimulus" from the Navy to develop an innovative private sector economy, the city has squandered time and money on a series of disjointed projects and endeavors that have not taken us out of this dependent state or raised our national profile. Instead the city has spent $78M of our money over the past five years buying land around the base to appease the Navy. [25] This land will not yield any rent or return. Currently the Navy is happy in Virginia Beach[26], but this view can change like the weather.

---

[25] Charlie Passut, Jet Base Could be in Play, *TidewaterNews.com* February 6, 2010

[26] Ibid

That being said, it is understandable that there must be compromises. However, instead of prolonging the cat and mouse games between the city and the Navy, the tax base monies gained from the military economy should be reinvested into educational, industrial and service infrastructure so that when the Navy leaves, these projects will be able to cover the city's losses.

We are living on borrowed time, and local government should be coming up with a long-term master plan The local government has smartly been improving long-term efficiency by investing in the light rail to connect Norfolk and Virginia Beach. However, there has to be an economic growth engine that will not just conserve resources but also draw them into our region.

I have been advocating by letter writing to local elected leaders over the past few years the idea of setting up a University of Virginia (UVA) or Virginia Tech (VT) satellite campus at our oceanfront. The counter-arguments which I received are that we already have Old Dominion, William and Mary and Regent University nearby. However, none of these schools are ranked as highly as UVA or VT. For cities to achieve greatness, they must have world-class academic institutions. The great cities all over the world have great schools: Boston has Harvard and MIT, New York has Cornell and NYU, Chicago has University of Chicago and Northwestern, Los Angeles has UCLA and USC, and so on.

The University of Virginia – Oceanfront Campus would be a series buildings set up along Atlantic and Pacific Avenue between 8th and 30th streets and also in the corridor between the Oceanfront and the Convention Center. Like Pepperdine in Malibu, University of

California in San Diego or Northwestern University in Chicago, we could create a scenic campus offering world-class education, while conducting cutting-edge research in science, medicine and the arts. Currently, this section of our oceanfront has a lot of low-revenue-generating businesses such as t-shirt shops and motels. I personally believe these establishments are devaluing our area as a whole.

Our area is ideally situated for a major research institution with close proximity to the military bases, NASA at Langley and the shipyards. These entities offer tremendous opportunity for innovation and new technology research. Our town can become an East Coast Silicon Valley. Seattle, San Francisco, LA, NY, Chicago, and Atlanta thrive in large part because they are able to create a talent pipeline to attract innovative companies.

Eminent domain is most appropriate for chartering a major research university that not only serves the local, state and national interests but also raises the revenue and business viability of our area. We are entering a knowledge-based economic era in which the money goes to those who innovate. We could create a local franchise of an already world-class brand by investing in the University of Virginia, ranked 2nd best public university in the United States, according to *U.S. News and World Report*. Moreover, the school is highly regarded in law, medicine, science and the arts. [27] The school is highly

---

[27]The University of Virginia, Facts at a Glance: virginia.edu/Facts/Glance_Rankings.html

selective, accepting only 5,760 of 14,824 undergraduate applicants, according to USA Today.

Moreover, the campus economy created from September to May would offset the seasonal decline in tourism in a healthy and sustainable manner.

Companies place strong consideration in workforce viability before relocating to an area. They need a reliable pipeline of skilled talent such as engineers, IT specialists and tradesman who are entering the local work force each year. The University of Virginia at the Oceanfront would offer this talent, which in turn would attract companies offering high-paying jobs. Much of Silicon Valley's success can be attributed to the proximity of Stanford and the University of California Berkley.

If such an economy were to take root, we would see property values rise while property taxes remain flat or even decline due to the increased inflow of corporate and sales tax revenue resulting from student consumption.

Moreover, the local military bases turn over a great deal of talent every year. Why not offer the exiting veterans a school with world-wide name recognition where they can use their GI Bill benefits to further their education while building our local economy? This would help us retain top military talent who will eventually lead the local companies and perhaps our city as well. Moreover, as our area becomes a center for R&D, the Navy may be more inclined to stay and invest more into the region. Nothing big happens unless bold moves are made by decisive and deliberate leaders. Such a transformation would be financially and politically costly. However, only grand-scale investment can transform our area from a sleepy beach town into a world-class center for innovation. Current property tax increases are due to the fact we have no other significant base from which to draw money to keep pace with inflation. Every year, costs rise: dredging the inlet, repairing roads, replacing sand on the beach. Thus, we either have to pay more taxes or cut services to keep the status quo. Implementing a grand vision would allow us to see our net worth rise through property appreciation while creating opportunities for newcomers in search of the American dream.

I was very excited about starting my new role in regional economic development; I felt I could actually contribute to the local economy by using my talents and experiences to help make our city and region great.

Economic Development

Many cities and counties throughout the nation have an Economic Development (ED) department to help attract outside companies to their area. There are also regional organizations, which in our case is a public-private partnership. The Hampton Roads region has both a regional economic development organization and fifteen city and county organizations within the region performing more or less the same function. Some are one-person operations, while others, such as Virginia Beach, Hampton and Norfolk, are layered organizations with a president, group of directors and internal staff. The regional organization receives around a dollar per resident from each of the member cities and counties, as well as membership fees from various private companies such as banks, law firms and real estate development companies.

There are several positions within a medium to large Economic Development organization: The CEO, who both runs the organization internally and represents the region externally; Marketing and Communications, which manages press releases and external communications; Investor Relations, which manages the relationships between the municipalities and the private companies that invest money into the organization; Business Outreach, which essentially calls companies for a meet-up; Operations Manager, which manages the IT systems and financials; Research Manager, which provides statistical data and information support to the marketing managers (my position); support staff; and Marketing Managers, the most interesting position of all.

Marketing Managers get to travel around the world to places like Chicago, New York, Israel, Korea, Japan, Germany and Poland to meet consultants and C-level executives (key corporate decision makers such as CEOs, COOs & CFOs), display the region at tradeshows, attend parties (known as "events") and even attend baseball games on occasion. I don't know much about the consultants other than that they are highly paid to schedule meetings with C-level executives for the Marketing Managers. I have heard that consultant fees range from $500 to $1000 or more per meeting.

The goal is to open businesses in the Hampton Roads area in one of the four priority areas: modeling and simulation; regional office and headquarters; distribution centers and light manufacturing; and aerospace and defense companies. Openings or hiring in the retail sector, such as Wal-Mart, Applebee's and Costco, do not count, since this sector generally services the population instead of creating high-value managerial, manufacturing and technical jobs.

During the interview process, I was told several times that I was "overqualified" to be a research manager, but nevertheless I felt perfectly qualified considering the times were in. Individuals, families, communities, and corporations have to do more with less. People are expecting more output with less investment. I was willing to work for well below what I made in previous jobs and still give them stellar output. Our region, although more resilient than most others nationally, was still reeling from the after-effects of the global financial crisis.

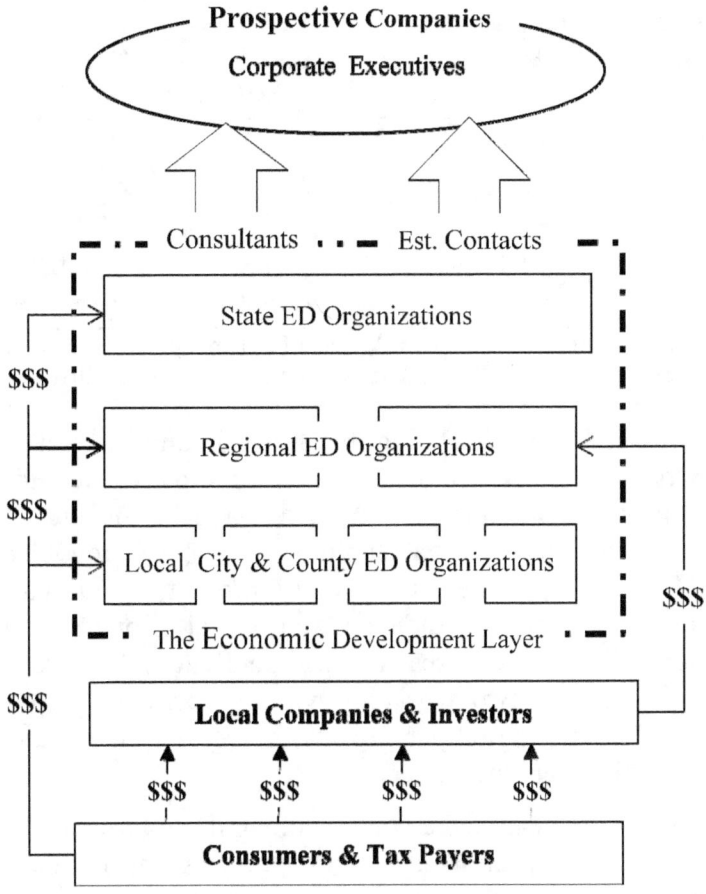

The Economic Development "Operating System"/Business Model: Taxpayers who are also consumers pay their local governments to attract job-creating investment to their area. However, within the Economic Development layer there exists redundancy that may hamper output. This is measured as new jobs created and/or total investment brought into the region.

Hampton Roads Region			
Year	Announcements - New Jobs	Closings - Jobs Lost	Net
2006	3,697	3,311	386
2007	3,316	1,246	2,070
2008	5,549	1,779	3,770
2009	2,875	5,265	**-2,390**
2010*	785	992	**-207**

Source: Virginia Economic Development Partnership: Resource Center/ Closings vs. Announcements Data (* as of May 28,2010)

I convinced them by stating that I could connect research and data to the end consumer, the company executive looking for a suitable location to expand his business. I emphasized that I am a Hampton Roads "shareholder" with a vested interest—I own property and have maintained both a residence and rental property (for which I have paid taxes to Virginia Beach) for over a decade. After a two week interview process, I accepted their offer of $55,000 per year, with two weeks' vacation and health insurance.

The past few years have been challenging in terms of job creation; we lost the Norfolk Ford motor plant that made F-150 pick-up trucks, and we also lost Lillian Vernon, a personalized gift merchant, when it announced it was ceasing operations in Virginia Beach by August 2011. Additionally, the highly publicized International Paper plant shut down in Franklin.

And with only four Fortune 500 headquarters (Amerigroup, Dollar Tree, Smithfield Foods and Norfolk Southern Railroad), our area is at great economic risk, being mostly dependent on the military. A colleague from another ED organization mentioned that it was difficult to attract and retain high-value workers if they feel "trapped" in an area. They may come to work for Amerigroup, but they may not be able to find work at another company if something goes wrong, or if they run out of room to advance.

Our area's ten largest employers are: the Department of Defense (DOD), Newport News Shipbuilding (which depends on DOD), Sentara Healthcare, City of Virginia Beach Schools, Wal-Mart, Norfolk Public Schools, The City of Virginia Beach, Chesapeake City Public Schools, Riverside Medical Center and Newport News Public Schools. Smithfield Foods is ranked 17th. Basically, our area's major employers are the government, hospitals and Wal-Mart, and our economy is mainly rooted in money spent at chain retailers and hospitals.[28]

There is a general macro-trend of European and Japanese companies looking to relocate operations to the U.S. due to their declining demographic picture, which is leading to a critical skills shortage – not enough young people with a technical education. The companies are drawn to America because of favorable taxes and a flexible workforce. Employment laws in the U.S. favor these companies much more than laws in Europe. In Japan, they are essentially losing their potential workforce because of low birth rates. Since many Japanese

---

[28] Virginia Employment Commission, MSA Community Profile: Virginia Beach – Norfolk, Newport News, VA-NC (VA Part) May 28, 2010 Update.

companies export most of their output, namely to the U.S., they find it easier to produce where the products are sold. Hence, ED organizations all over the country are courting these companies and trying to convince them that their location is the most suitable location.

The first day on the job started with an uneventful meeting, where I was introduced to the regional organization and "heads of state" from the localities. Afterward I was assigned not to a cubicle but to an actual office with a stunning view of downtown Norfolk and the USS Wisconsin Battleship. For a brief moment, I felt like I was back at Pärnu Mnt 15, where I had a view of Toompea, a medieval castle tower in Tallinn, Estonia. Then I noticed a strange picture on the adjacent office door which surprised me: three color laser print-outs of a congested Indian slum with a telephone pole supporting a mishmash of wires. Underneath the picture was written: "This is India; it's where you call when you have a technical problem with your computer" (the pictures are posted at: Facebook.TheOrganicStimulusPlan.com). To my amazement, this was posted on the door by a colleague who had been employed by this organization for a long time. It was quite unbelievable that an organization would allow such pictures to be displayed. I was stunned, but I did not want to rock the boat on my first day.

During my first week, a colleague and I went on a road trip to see some empty buildings in Suffolk. During the drive, we were making small talk, and he mentioned that my job was a great job to "milk". I responded that I wanted to do well at the company and make some sort of impact, so that my property values would go up. I explained that property prices are generally a function of scarcity and income in the given area. If we could get more people with high-paying jobs into the area quickly, the housing supply would suddenly go into shortage, causing house prices to go up and raising existing home owners' equity. But through our conversation, I got the impression that my new job had very little to do with economics and more to do with petty politics between our organization and others within the Economic Development layer. It was all about meeting "great guys" and "building that relationship". I was told, "If people like you, they will work with you, and if they don't like you, they will just put your request at the bottom of the pile" – nothing to do with working towards a common goal of creating jobs during dire times. I wrongly assumed that if everyone was on the same page and our mission was focused (serving the taxpayers by doing our part to bring more jobs and ultimately more wealth to our region) that the relationships would be easy to build. I thought we would be judged on our abilities instead of our small talk skills, much like the operational military culture. I find it generally difficult to build relationships with those who are lazy or have hidden agendas.

During the interview process and early discussions with management, I got the impression that more was expected of me than just copying and pasting information from key governmental websites to emails or our homepage. I was also to take charge of running REMI PI+, a computer model that simulates the effects of changes made to workforce and industry dynamics within our region. They told me I was brought on board to help them think differently. I was especially attuned to the fact we were handling taxpayers' money, and I wanted to do my part to make sure that they were getting the most out of their investment in me. Within the first week, I saw immediate opportunities to make a significant improvement in productivity and provide data that would uniquely differentiate our region.

One of our tasks was to take demographic data from various sources, put this data into a spreadsheet, and then paste it into the website via the content management system. This was an arduous task, but I knew this process could be automated with some database programming (which I didn't know how to do, unfortunately). I crafted a very specific business requirement document and hoped we could recruit a management information systems (MIS) student from one of the state universities for a summer internship, giving him an opportunity to gain work experience while we got automated. This would, I thought, save substantial amounts of taxpayer money both upfront and down the line with increased productivity. This rather simple concept, however, was looked upon by the management as too fantastic or far-fetched, and nothing became of it

The second item that concerned me was a problem statement that I received during the interviews: Approximately 15,000 service members separate from the military in Hampton Roads every year, according to a study by Virginia Beach ED. We wanted to figure out how to attract the ones with engineering degrees for companies that visited and operate within the region; these companies often inquired of us where they could get a highly skilled engineering work force. I knew from my experience as a former Junior Military Officer (JMO) that there are a substantial amount of young military officers with engineering degrees. In fact, recruiters who specialize in placing JMOs host events at the Embassy Suites in Hampton a few times every year.

But JMOs are slipping out of here in droves; the best way to keep them here is to offer them high-paying jobs. Most JMOs are quite versatile and willing to move anywhere for the right job and salary. Thus, our goal was to first determine how many JMOs with engineering degrees are exiting the military every year, and then present this data to prospective companies. I did my own estimates and found that we may have a few hundred engineers exiting the military who went to top schools like Annapolis, Ohio State, Virginia Tech and University of Illinois; these JMOs have "hands-on" engineering and management work experience. However, I wanted to get more exact data direct from the DOD.

It was suggested that I should befriend someone in the Pentagon and ask for this data as a favor. I tried not to laugh.

If such military separation data (exit location, skills, degrees and years of service) could be provided for every region in the country, it could in fact help the nation as a whole attract more foreign manufacturers from Germany, Japan and Canada. Manufacturing and technology companies consider access to engineering talent when deciding on new locations, and showing them the number of viable job candidates in our area could help convince them to open branches in Virginia. Such business intelligence would strengthen the American economy if applied nationally. Moreover, the military could use this data as a pitch for the recruitment of highly talented people, essentially saying, "If you want to become a leader at GE, Pfizer, Dow Chemical and or KPMG, then join the Navy—you can hone your technical skills, save money for your MBA, and develop your leadership abilities, all while serving your country."

To get such data would require more than buying a sandwich for a Pentagon staffer. It would require deliberate effort; the Governor and Congressional delegations would have to discuss the matter with the Secretary of Defense to make a census-like database available to local governments, or even to the public. To actually set this up is relatively easy. It is a matter of formulating an Oracle or SQL query which can be programmed to automatically update every year. But instead of enthusiasm, what I found was apathy, an unwillingness to even listen to my ideas in their entirety. My proposal to have an IT/MIS intern automate mundane, low value processes was interpreted as laziness on my part. But automating the easy yet time-consuming tasks would allow us more time to crack the riddle of the military separation data, which would help lure significant companies to our area; it would also give us more time to phone prospective companies for appointments.

We as taxpayers lose when we employ high-level managers and executives who do not, at the very least, have a basic understanding of how technology and IT increases productivity. Case in point: a website contracted by one of the organizations within the ED layer cost well over $40,000, plus ongoing costs (which I suspect were in the range of $100 per hour). This could, however, have been done by students at a nearby college for a fraction of the cost. A website of this cost should have a database on the backend that automatically imports city data from an excel spreadsheet, then manipulates and formats this demographic and workforce information for each locality in a standardized uniform manner.

A few weeks later, I decided to skip an "optional" reception for Mayor Fraim, which was taking place around 5 pm. I came in an hour early that day and decided to leave fifteen minutes early to avoid rush hour traffic; my wife had the day off, and I really wanted to see her. The following day, another colleague called me into her office. "We have an issue," she told me. "Someone in the office was very upset that you left early yesterday." I asked who it was, but she wouldn't say. I was learning what it was to be a public sector bureaucrat

The following week, I met with a small town ED department that was very welcoming and open to new ideas. It impressed me that they were trying to develop a master plan first, and then bring in appropriate businesses. We had a discussion about the budgetary problems, and I proposed the idea that police departments and other services should be merged, at least administratively, to save money while maintaining officer headcount at current levels. The head of this ED department was open to the idea and told me that they recently merged their 911 services with another community, reaping substantial savings.

Cities and counties within Hampton Roads depend on each other: people live in one town, work in another and shop in yet another. In fact, ODU Professor and Regional Economist Dr. James Koch had recently published a report showing that regionalization exists: a dollar invested in one community yields return in almost all the others, and vice versa. During one of my visits, I wanted to discuss this topic as it pertained to our times and affected our daily lives.

However, many of my colleagues from both my organization and our partner ED organizations appeared oblivious to the fact that we were in the middle of an economic crisis, with many of our cities and counties using Federal stimulus money to make ends meet.[29] The regional organization receives taxpayer money and, indirectly, federal stimulus money. Yet, it appeared that there was no sense of urgency. Of the $787 billion allocated for the American Recovery and Reinvestment Act of 2009, $399 billion has already been spent as of May 31, 2010 according to Recovery.gov, the official U.S. government website for stimulus reporting. I was advised not to take my job too seriously, that we were just a marketing organization.

In my heart, I found this attitude disgusting, considering the fact that communities are even contemplating cutbacks in schools and police forces to balance budgets. The city of Gloucester, Virginia, for example, cut the school year from 180 to 160 days to help make up for a $1.8 million dollar budget shortfall. The community is also contemplating a four-day school week option for next year. [30]

---

[29] The Virginian-Pilot, Stimulus Money Mired in Red Tape, March 22, 2010.

[30] Wavy TV-10, Gloucester to Shorten School Year, April 29, 2010

I expressed my opinion that although the hours would be made up by adding a few minutes to the school day, the town runs the risk of being perceived as having questionable public education, which ultimately leads to a decline in property values. In a meeting, I brought up the fact that we must find ways to become more efficient and increase output, as taxpayers are on edge about their jobs and the future. I felt they were looking to ED to bring them jobs.

Perhaps this collective attitude of obstinance, sloth and pettiness accumulated over time has led to the economic stagnation within our region. Although we are doing better than other regions because of our military sector, which provides steady employment during tough times, we are not really advancing. Our unemployment rates may be lower than the national average, but they are still elevated. Our housing prices are mostly stagnant, and we are facing the realities of job cuts. Furthermore, doing better these days is defined as not doing as badly as others.

The Brookings Institute released a report in May 2010 stating that Hampton Roads is "one of the most demographically disadvantaged regions," lumping us with Detroit and Buffalo[31]. In one meeting a colleague joked that we were "The Detroit of the mid-Atlantic." Although I was offended by the report and saw it as a threat to my property value, I could not disagree. The report rated regions on immigration, education, aging and

---

[31] Megan Hoyer, Old, Slow and not too bright. Welcome to Hampton Roads, The Virginian-Pilot, May 9, 2010

transportation. My wife, an immigrant, is finding it difficult to make friends to whom she can relate; there is constant traffic in the Hampton Roads Bridge-Tunnel; and I felt it was next to impossible to explain anything technical to my colleagues. The report stated that these factors would hamper growth and emphasized how the key factors to growth were educational attainment and diversity. The report touted Seattle, Washington DC, San Antonio and Denver as the "Next Frontier Regions." Local leadership has been consumed with turf battles, forgetting to enable us for a future where resources will be scarcer and competition more fierce.

But expressing strong opinions that challenged the status-quo was not appreciated as thinking differently. I was called into my boss's office after returning from Richmond, where I had had productive meetings with the state organization on how to automate mundane data collection not only for our region, but all other organizations in the state. My boss wanted to fire me. He maintained that I did not know how to work in a "public-private partnership nonprofit organization." But I knew who paid my salary at the end of the day – the people of Hampton Roads. In the private sector, lack of innovation is self-corrected by competitors or declining profits. Sadly, this is not the case in the public sector.

I am not sure why public-private partnerships need to be different from any other organization. There is no reason why we should relegate government or related organizations to sloth and apathy. Our mission is quite simple--to promote Hampton Roads. This is measured by how many new jobs are created and how many total dollar investments are made. The jobs create wealth, and in turn new employees spend locally, boosting the economy.

I managed to save my job that day and also demanded that the degrading pictures on my colleague's door be removed. I came home that day with a terrible look on my face. My wife was shocked. The anxiety from these episodes created a lot of uncertainty, and I felt bad that I could not make promises to my wife about the future. Instead of planning for the best, we were preparing for the worst. Discretionary spending ceased, and we started to take measures to save at every opportunity. I decided to play the game while contemplating the future.

My early perceptions of ED were soon confirmed; the job had very little to do with developing the economy and more to do with keeping things cool with others within the *economic development layer*. Government jobs, whether federal, state, local or public/private nonprofits should be the perfect places for people to suggest innovative changes. Forum and debate bring problems to light before they occur. However, this mentality appeared non-existent. It appeared that private sector experience had no equivalency or meaning inside the *economic development layer*. I was supposed to keep my nose down and only speak up after I have established myself as a bureaucrat.

The following week, the success metrics were finally explained to me in detail over a lunch at a nearby steakhouse (paid for by the taxpayers). Essentially, our organization was supposed to meet a lot of people, but we were ultimately not accountable for the outcomes; the local ED organizations had to close the deals. Hence, I perceived that this organization's only purpose was to spend money. But when this happens for a long period of time, those involved tend to forget who is paying.

I noticed there were a lot of events where one ED organization would host another ED organization. Instead of convincing companies why they should move to Hampton Roads, it appeared that our time and even money was spent instead trying to convince each other that we need to work together.

I got a bit of respite when I attended formal training for REMI PI+ in Amherst, Massachusetts. There, I met highly educated people who studied and even taught economics, engineering and mathematics. Although Amherst was a small town, it felt like a big city, as the people were very diverse and open minded. Upon my return I was full of vigor and hope that I could actually do some "real value added work". I wanted to use the model I learned about in Amherst to determine the increase in potential tax revenue if a company within a certain sector located to our region. It could also predict job creation, both direct and indirect. In essence, such a program could tell you how many hairstylist positions would be created if you created a new manufacturing facility that employed fifty people. The program would also tell you the rise in the value of capital stock, which is the rise in taxable property. This output data helps localities determine the level of incentives to offer a prospective company. Upon my return from Amherst, the boss was leaving for Korea. , and I headed to Washington DC for The Council for Community Research Conference (C2ER) just as he returned from Korea. This conference was more interesting than I expected. Both governmental agencies and private companies lectured about new sources of data that would be helpful in community development. I also attended a seminar by Next Generation Consulting called "How Cool Is Your City?" which affirmed the Brookings Institute Study released a few weeks earlier: areas with diversity and tolerance, good transportation and highly educated people is where the young high tech, managerial and skilled workers want to be. [32]

On the last day, there was a special early morning meeting for those of us who collected pricing data for the cost of living (COLI) index which compares by city and region the cost of food, housing, utilities, medical care, etc. I was happily dozing through this ordeal until I was approached by a lady who was a research manager from southwestern Virginia. She stated that the Virginia contingent wasn't as strong as usual and remarked that she and I were "competitors". She felt that we are competing for the same companies and a win for one city meant a loss for another. I had the opposite view. In fact, I believed, if a company locates to one city, it would spur demand from suppliers in others.

Another ED worker from my region appeared receptive as I discussed my concerns that there are too many politics and rituals getting in the way of producing meaningful data. I told her we could perhaps automate the key demographic figures and produce a database that all ED organizations could access. But from the reactions of my colleagues, I got the idea that many people who have been in government for a long time view passion, vision, drive

---

[32] Ibid

and determination as a threat, not as key attributes necessary to building our nation.

The trip to DC made my wife and I realize that we needed to move to a big city where we could enjoy diversity, nightlife and progressive thinking. In such a city, there are more meaningful jobs with a better chance of upward promotion. During some off hours at the conference, we went to the National Zoo, where we discovered that Panda bears like popsicles, specially prepared by zoologists. Imagining similar interesting experiences every weekend, our resolve to move was strengthened.

The week after returning from DC, I was called into my boss's office late one afternoon. He had his assistant sitting next to him taking notes. He gave me what appeared to be a pre-rehearsed speech, given to him by a lawyer, that I was not meeting expectations and not been able to do the work (although a week earlier, he had complimented me on a business model I helped create for the Korean companies). I was offered a "special severance" package of $3200, the after-tax equivalent of four weeks' pay. This severance, offered for only three months of work, felt like a victory in the sense that I was perhaps being bought off. I decided after this and the previous experience that I would stop banging my head against the wall with these small town jobs and get back to my roots in IT by studying to update my skills and pursuing work in a major metropolitan area.

From this experience, I came away with the notion that perhaps if the various state, regional and local organizations' functions were aligned with the needs of the customers (the taxpayers and the executives at the prospective companies we are courting), we may see better results. I believe that the current set of redundancies within the Economic Development Layer creates internal competition and pettiness that absorbs many dollars and diverts time away from the development of the economy. There are a number of overlapping positions that could be removed to cut costs, and moving from premium city office buildings to others may also be an effective cost-saving measure.

In my opinion, the current structure creates resistance to consolidation and technological innovation, because it threatens the existence of those in charge. This problem originates with the fact that various ED organization are set up in such way that there is no single leader to break ties, settle internal squabbles or create a unified vision. The absence of unified leadership leads to the formation of factions within these fragmented organizations that squabble among themselves instead of working for the common good. This type of behavior is prevalent in tribal and lawless regions in third-world countries. This is especially damaging because strong local leadership is so badly needed, having more of an impact on our daily lives than on national leadership.

Moreover, consolidation will strengthen the ED workforce. We may see ourselves as several different organizations, but clients likely see us as one big one, and would appreciate a unified approach. It would be better if economic development was unified at the state level, consolidating leadership, sales and marketing, research, data and IT. We would then only need regional experts to keep up with available land sites and each region's unique existing and emerging attributes.

The resulting savings would not only reduce the strain on municipal budgets, but it would also allow for the state to hire fewer (higher quality and perhaps more ambitious) employees who will deliver the results we need to survive when stimulus is gone—innovative, outspoken and creative leaders instead of par-for-the-course public servants. I would logically deduce that the best people to interface with corporate executives are ones who were corporate executives themselves. A unified and consolidated organization could afford a Fortune 500 executive who may be looking to "give back" as an ED CEO or Chief Marketing Officer. Additionally, such a person would have a healthy rolodex of potential contacts, reducing the need for consultants.

With all the efforts we are making to attract Asian companies, it is logical that an ED organization needs to hire top-tier MBAs who speak Japanese, Korean and Chinese. Consolidation would allow us to afford a core team of these corporate elites to represent our state, region and municipalities abroad.

When a region's ED representatives visit Japan, for example, to meet with Toyota or Mitsubishi, the opening introduction can be given by a highly educated, well respected accomplished business executive; this will show more respect for a CEO's position than an introduction by a career public servant. Follow-on presentations could be given by marketing managers who speak the client's language. This way, the executive gets the impression that we are serious, unified and qualified to help his company succeed.

If the Tea Party wants a tangible cause, this is it. By requesting to see the budgets of town and county departments, they may discover overlaps in resources which waste valuable time and money. Right now there are a lot of people high on emotion, fire and passion, but short on step-wise plans. If the Tea Party can present proper business plans for how they plan to reorganize local and state government in the most efficient manner possible, perhaps they can actually fix problems in a measurable way.

PART II - THE SITUATION

America

Despite the headlines, our country still remains the most desirable place to live. Although the economy is in a recession, there is no shortage of foreigners still hoping for a shot at the American Dream. Our ability to attract ambitious and intelligent workers, and then assimilate these forces into our culture remains our unique strength. While there is no truly common American identity, there exists a common mentality of working together to achieve tangible results. Our nation will undoubtedly continue to be a dominant economic force and remain, on a per capita basis, among the richest nations on earth. The melting pot effect and our ability to judge people on merit instead of lineage have made us the most innovative country in the world. For example, the United States, with approximately 5% of the world's population, creates almost half the world's patents[33]. Our greatest strength is not only our ability to adjust to the constantly changing environment but also to overcome impossible odds. A Finnish friend of mine once said that America is like a cat—no matter how high you toss it in the air, it always lands on all four feet.

However, people are not happy. Recent polls suggest that 75% of Americans are unhappy with the way the government is handling the current state of affairs. It seems people are losing faith not just in a single party but

---

[33] US Patent and Trademark Office Patents By Country, State, and Year - Utility Patents, December 2008

in all[34]. A generation ago, graduating college usually meant a good job and a reasonable standard of living with a decent quality of life. Now we need two incomes just to buy a condo. People are angry, frustrated and confused.

Headline Grabbing & Regurgitation appears to be the latest national pastime—people read something in the paper, then repeat it at the coffee shop as if they are running for office. I used to do this myself until I realized it was just like chewing the fat. I would be better off doing my own research and writing a book.

People will read an article or hear a sound bite, then believe it completely as fact. But the writers of the headlines usually spin the article one way or another to fit a bias. Instead of thinking for themselves, most people are looking for a ready-made ideology to which to subscribe. The problem is that most of these ideologies are built on superficial one-liners, sound bites and cliché phrases:

"We're against big government"

"Go Green"

"Organic"

"Say no to taxes"

"Say no to spending"

"We support small business"

---

[34] Poll: Americans Angry At Washington; Palin Losing Support, MyStateLine.com, February 11, 2010

These days, most Americans are caught up in the 55+ hour work week, not to mention family obligations and all the mundane tasks like laundry and cutting grass. It appears that there is not much time for do-it-yourself analysis anymore. Most Americans just want to turn their brains off, relax and outsource the deep thinking to some guy on TV. The problem is that the purveyors of these ready-made ideologies, those delegated to do the thinking for us, are either mostly clueless when it comes to real solutions or have discovered that extreme emotions lead to good business. They offer us websites, rallies, t-shirts, coffee mugs and bashing – all the stuff we want to buy but don't really need.

I try to listen to Rush Limbaugh, but it's impossible. Instead of offering alternatives, compromise or solutions, he excels by fueling his listeners' anger. On the other extreme is Michael Moore; while he does offer some solutions, they are usually superficial and vague blanket statements. These people belong to an industry that feeds on perpetuating emotion.

Marketers have been capitalizing on emotion for as long as marketing and advertising have existed, capturing the moment while our guard is down to sells us something we really don't need. It can be clothes, hamburgers, shoes, mobile phones that have guitar strings on them. But the most profitable items to market are ideas and emotion, which don't require much overhead.

Among young people, I have observed a growing trend in the "cool to be stupid" attitude. My wife tells me that the people she meets at work brag about having DUIs and smoking marijuana. But none of this is actually cool. I used to hear from pot-heads that all the smart people at top schools and top companies smoke weed. Perhaps this explains the recent economic unwinding which has been attributed to the greed and selfish behavior among financial and corporate elites? [35]

The recent British Petroleum (BP) disaster in the Gulf of Mexico that claimed 11 lives and at this writing is still pouring millions of gallons of crude oil into the Gulf, resulting in one of the largest oil spills in history, illustrates what happens when corporate greed collides with government apathy. According to industry officials, the oil well blowout was caused by a methane gas bubble shooting up the drill column of the well, which burst through several seals before igniting and later exploding. Usually the pipes are filled with drilling mud, a heavier-than-water compound, to keep down the pressure; but instead the managers decided to use sea water. Later investigations found that the U.S. Minerals Management Service (MMS), the agency that oversees offshore drilling, was investigating claims that essential records, crucial to emergency management and platform shutdown, were not being kept up-to-date by BP.[36] Moreover, findings reveal that the government considered but did not actually end up requiring remote shut-off switches, which are already mandated in Norway and Brazil, that would allow crews to shut down oil flow

---

[35] Stuart Fox, What Causes Corporate Greed?, *Live Science*, April 29, 2010

[36] Beth Adelson, Troubling Details Emerge About BP's Oil Rig Explosion and Spill, *Government Accountability Project – Whistleblower.org*, April 29, 2010.

remotely even if the rig was damaged or sunken as in the current crisis. Experts advocate that such remote shut-off devices would have averted this disaster.

The U.S. oil industry protested these switches on the basis of cost and argued successfully that their backup systems were adequate. In fact, BP and other oil producers successfully pushed for voluntary regulation. The MMS had in effect allowed the industry to make and follow its own rules.[37] The "industry" as we hear it called in headlines, are mostly older educated men in their early 40s to late 60s making tens of millions of dollars per year. No one questions their intelligence or work ethic, but I find myself asking what went wrong that they would, in effect, take the "brakes off the car" to enhance performance? We will all be paying the price for this debacle for decades to come.

We also witnessed such corporate disconnect in the AIG scandal, which cost taxpayers $182 billion[38] when a small group of derivative traders decided to take liberties with the whole company, making risky - highly leveraged trades that if and they did went the wrong way, would take down the whole company.[39] Somewhere, the education process must teach our future leaders that when one takes from the system, one must ultimately return the

---

[37] Ibid

[38] Ronald D Orol, Geithner, Paulson defend $182 billion AIG bailout, *Marketwatch*, Jan 27, 2010

[39] Diane Brady, Marcia Vickers & Mike McNamee, AIG: What Went Wrong, *Businessweek*, April 11, 2010

same amount, and that certain decisions affect not only groups of people but society as a whole.

Single Majority

Technological advances are not only advancing our lives and improving our quality of life; they are transforming the social dynamic as well. Since the introduction of the PC and internet, our lives have changed in almost every aspect. At the core of this change is faster communication, leading to faster task completion. We can respond to inquiries and solve problems much more quickly than before. We can quickly expand our networks, and we have more choice than ever before. Essentially, technology presents more choices but with less time to decide, hence the information and sensory overload.

Instead of reaping the benefits of automation in the form of more free time, we are getting busier and thus finding ourselves becoming more removed from society as a whole. Some of the busiest people in the world are those in technology, working long hours on a routine basis. As our quality of life improves, our priorities change. Many people feel they must obtain a certain level of success before "settling down" or perhaps those basics have become harder to get.

In 2005, singles became the majority, according to U.S. Census data. Matchmaking businesses are popping up everywhere. Companionship is a basic human need that has been overlooked in this new era. I am sure loneliness is the root of much of the frustration and anxiety these days. From my experience, I can say that while I was single, I was not as focused; I was pre-occupied instead with "the game". I believe that marriage is as at least as important as getting an education and accumulating wealth,[40] and I am not sure why it is not emphasized anymore. Since my marriage, I have seen a rise in my creative energy, an improvement in my health as my wife and I cook together instead of eating fast food, a decline in my entertainment expenses, and an increase in my savings.

But corporations recognize that single people are more profitable for big business, because they spend more:

- They are more likely to eat out.

- They will buy drinks for themselves and others more readily.

- Singles will spend more on clothes and cars to attract a potential partner.

- Two single people living apart in separate apartments spend more than a married couple under one roof.

- Singles will work longer hours to pay for their lifestyles.

In essence, this may be why we see more TV shows glamorizing single life and downplaying married life. We see columnists and TV therapists telling us to be selective about our partners in an effort to keep us single longer so that we consume more. We see divorces being glamorized and hear about marriage causing depression. The average age for marriage rose from 22/24.7

---

[40] Linda J. Waite, The Importance of MARRIAGE Is Being Overlooked, USA Today (The Society for the Advancement of Education), January 1999

(male/female) in 1990 to 26/27.7 in 2007[41]. It is my impression that people who marry young are highly criticized

According the World Health Organization (WHO), the risk of developing depression among singles and divorced people is 2-4 times higher than among family people. Depression includes loss of interest or pleasure, feelings of guilt or low self-worth, disturbed sleep or appetite, low energy, and poor concentration. But this too is "good for business": 6% of the U.S. population (13 million people) was prescribed an antidepressant in 1996. This figure rose to more than 10% (27 million people) by 2005. [42] If we don't get a handle on this, we could end up incapacitated as a society. The World Health Organization estimates that depression is the main reason for absence from work and is rated second among incapacitating illnesses after the flu. Essentially the root causes of depression are loneliness and isolation from familiar people who offer us emotional support. Our policy must promote family. It must also support and encourage the needs of the American family ahead of corporate needs. Although the average work week has not changed that much since 1967, the average commute time continues to rise around the nation. Thus, this lost time is creating new anxiety and societal pressures. If we keep placing business needs ahead of family needs, we may end up with neither good

---

[41] US Census Bureau, American Community Survey

[42] Reuters, Use of antidepressant drugs in U.S. rising fast, August 3, 2009

families nor good businesses, as the depression epidemic may incapacitate the workforce.

To sustain long-term growth, businesses and society as a whole must invest in the people that support them. Squeezing people for a prolonged period of time while neglecting their human needs can only, in logical terms, lead to a crash. Even farmers know that you can't grow crops on the same land year after year. Periodically, they rotate crops or let the land sit fallow, replenishing its nutrients. This way the farmer is able to sustain yields indefinitely.

Hypocritical Conservatives

If the conservatives are really "in line with Jesus," as they claim, then let us see them vote this way. If they were truly interested in family values, they would advocate for shorter work-weeks and longer vacation time so workers can spend more time with our families. Study after study shows that the more time a family spends together, the greater their emotional stability, health and achievement.[43]

In gaining more family time, our work would become more meaningful. Corporate leaders, instead of taking massive and disproportionately large bonuses, would invest in hiring and developing their people. If conservatives push for the well being of the middle class, everyone will benefit as a whole. The wealthy will have a better work force and the poor will have more opportunities to lift themselves up. True conservatives should be pushing for the well-being of the working class family, not the CEO's family.

Naturally Declining Abortion

The conservatives play on people's religious values to win support. The abortion issue, for example, is often used to manipulate voters. The truth is that abortion has been declining steadily; the biggest drop was actually during the Clinton years, when our country was in the midst of an unprecedented economic boom.

---

[43] Susan Henry, Families that Eat Together Stay Together, *Sportzwire*, April 4, 2000

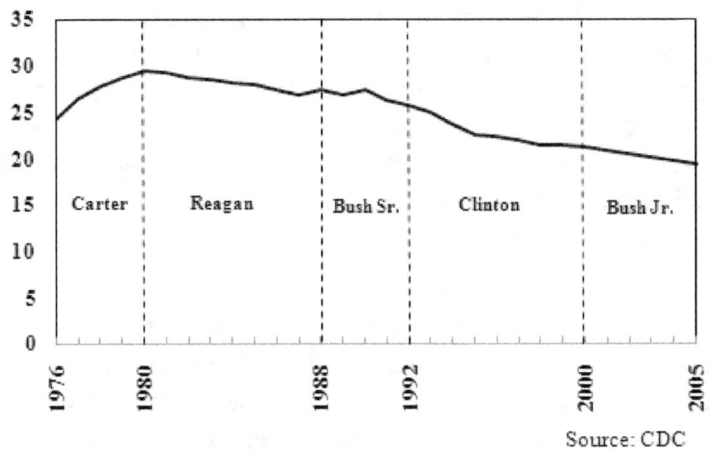

ABORTION RATE PER 1000 PREGNANCIES

Source: CDC

I am personally against abortion, which makes me for programs that offer prospective single mothers alternatives and support. During my high school years, I used to hang out with a Catholic group that purchased and renovated halfway homes for unwed mothers. However, many of these projects were developed in well-to-do areas, not the poor areas where they were greatly needed.

Abortion is a reluctant decision, made often out of shame, economic worry, or lack of family support. In a recent survey of women who had abortion, nearly three-fourths cited economic hardship as a reason for obtaining an abortion; three-fourths also cited having a child as interfering with work or school.[44] Moreover, single mothers and those who have children outside of marriage

---

[44] Tom Roberts, Study: Woman, Family Support Linked To Abortion Rate Drop, *National Catholic Reporter,* August 27, 2008

tend to be stigmatized in our society. We should spend our money helping them rather than berating them. Essentially, being pro-life means more than just rallies and shouting on TV. It means investing in a policy that allows people to be with their families in times of need. Let us not forget that founding fathers Thomas Paine and Alexander Hamilton, Renaissance man Leonardo da Vinci, and countless other individuals of stature were born out of wedlock.

A study of public policy from 1982 to 2000 discovered that programs not normally associated with reducing abortions had a noted effect on the rate of abortion from one state to another. For instance, the Welfare Reform Act of 1996 allowed states to impose a cap on the number of children eligible to receive economic assistance in low-income families. The study found that removing the cap did not increase fertility rates. Instead, according to the study, removing the cap decreased abortions by 15%, or 150,000, on a nationwide basis. Also, the findings indicate that during the 1990s the states with more generous grants to women, infants and children under the age of 5 resulted in a 37% lower abortion rate. Moreover, higher male employment during that decade was associated with a 29% lower abortion rate. [45]

The Democrats for Life proposed the Pregnant Women's Support Act on April 21, 2009 (HR Bill 2035) which introduces public policy and social programs that aim to lower the abortion rate in America. This group aspires to develop solutions on shared values between both parties:

---

[45] Ibid

building up the American family for the greater good of the nation as a whole. The status of this bill can be tracked on www.govtrack.us.

Death Penalty: The Cost of Revenge

According to Matthew 5:38-42, there is a difference between justice and revenge. God has given us some legitimate avenues for earthly justice, it tells us, but Jesus warned us that personal revenge is completely different. While revenge may taste sweet, it's wrong. Romans 12.17-21 further cautions about the thirst for justice turning into a quest for revenge.

Our law enforcement system is meant to remove and isolate the threat from society in a cost-efficient manner. Security forces are an expense. We don't gain any return by jailing criminals; in fact it is a cost. A person that could be earning $45,000 per year - about the U.S. average -- is now costing our society on average around $30,000 per year to keep him removed from society[46]. On the other hand, schools and infrastructure programs are an investment, yielding a greater return than the initial investment over an extended timeline. Kids who go through the public education system end up paying the system back through income taxes later in their lives.

From a cost perspective, the death penalty is tremendously expensive:

- In California, confining an inmate to death row costs $90,000 more per year (due to extra legal fees) than

---

[46] Bureau of Justice Statistics: http://bjs.ojp.usdoj.gov/

sentencing him to life without parole in a maximum security prison. With California's current death row population of 670, that accounts for $63.3 million annually.[47]

1,266 teachers could have been hired in California for this price.

- Maryland spent a total of $186M for five death penalty cases from 1982 to 1999 ($37.2 million for each execution). The study estimates that the average cost to Maryland taxpayers for reaching a single death sentence is $3 million - $1.9 million more than the cost of a non-death penalty case. This includes investigation, trial, appeals, and incarceration costs.[48]

To execute five criminals who were already removed from society cost Maryland an extra $10.9M per year during the study's 17 year time period. 273 teachers could have been hired at $40,000 per year for the same time period.

- New Jersey spent more than $250M from 1983 to 2005 on a capital punishment system that has executed no one. Since 1982, there have been 197 capital trials and 60 death sentences, of which 50 were

---

[47] California Commission on the Fair Administration of Justice, June 30, 2008

[48] The Cost of the Death Penalty in Maryland, *The Urban Institute*, March 2008

reversed. There have been no executions, although 10 men are currently housed on the state's death row. [49]

A quarter of a billion dollars spent over 23 years on 197 already-removed criminals costs about $11M per year. This equates to 220 new teachers with an annual salary of $50,000 each.

- The Federal Government spent $1.6B more on capital trials from 1982-1997 than on life imprisonment. Counties manage these high costs by decreasing funding for highways and police and by increasing taxes. [50]

This equates to hiring almost 1100 college professors at $100,000 per year for the 25-year period.

Ultimately, the death penalty doesn't work. The states with the death penalty have more crime than the ones without capital punishment, according to the FBI and U.S. Census data. This is the price of revenge.

---

[49] Mary E. Forsberg, Money for Nothing, *New Jersey Policy Perspective*, November 2005

[50] Katherine Baicker, The Budgetary Repercussions of Capital Convictions, The National Bureau of Economic Research (Paper 8382), July 2001

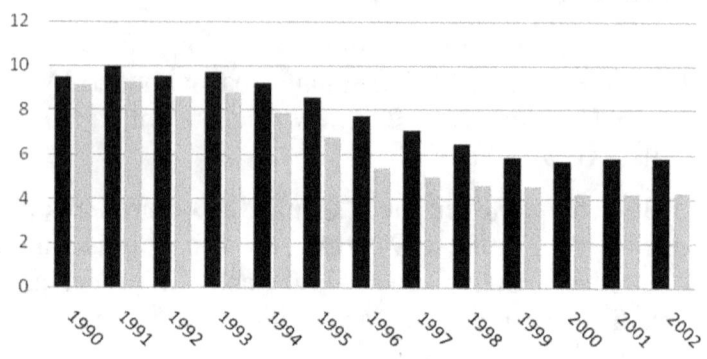

Murder Rate per 100,000 vs. Capital Punishment

■ Murder Rate in Death Penalty States ▨ Murder Rate in Non Death Penalty States

Source: FBI, US Census Bureau

Capital Punishment Does Not Deter Crime

The benefactors of the death penalty are mostly the lawyers and law firms associated with these cases.[51] Politicians, too, benefit from their support of the death penalty. Instead of confronting the root causes of violence, politicians offer the death penalty as if it were a meaningful solution to crime. They do this, however, at the expense of vital community services.

We elect people who should be smarter than the rest of us to separate emotions from facts before making a decision. Politicians should enlighten and inform us about the realities of the death penalty But instead we keep electing people on their superficial qualifications.

---

[51] USCourts.gov http://www.uscourts.gov/dpenalty/4REPORT.htm

The reality of the law is that we have to work within the confines of the U.S. Constitution. It is the basis of our nation's existence. Ultimately, there is no way to cut court costs for the death penalty beyond removing it completely. Our society has limited time and money but unlimited needs and wants. Instead of helping us find a balance, the conservatives have distracted us with what amounts to a whole lot of nothing.

Greenwashed Liberals

Most liberals are pleasant people, many of whom don't fit into the mainstream and define themselves by creative pursuits. Interestingly enough, the liberals whom I have encountered tend to be from wealthier white American families, with excellent educations. The ones I have met, however, are fascinated by life in third-world countries while having never spent a day there. Like conservatives, they tend to be as extreme in their beliefs. Perhaps this explains the 50/50 split[52] that results in no major accomplishments in government. The conservatives want everyone in the world to live like Americans, and the liberals don't want anyone to live like Americans. Liberals indirectly argue that the rest of the world should never aspire to our wealth, while they themselves get to live in modern condos, eat expensive strawberries and drive Volkswagens. They don't accept that people in other parts of the world want and should be able to attain comforts as well.

Organic Consumerism

The organic movement is full of good intentions but short on logic. The premise of the organic movement is to employ small farmers and food artisans who minimize the use of chemicals and additives. This supposedly improves nutrition and taste. However, there are serious consequences related to "going organic."

---

[52] Times/CBS News Survey: General Electorate is Evenly Split. April 20, 2010.

On Sundays, I promote my cookies at the locally-owned food and farmers' markets. Generally, most of the clientele is liberal. When they ask me if my products are organic, I tell them no, but they are made with some organic ingredients. Then they ask me if my cookies are Fair Trade. This means that the ingredients originate from farms where workers are being treated fairly. I tell them such ingredients would make our products cost prohibitive to the general public. Are you willing to pay $5 for one cookie?

I even had a customer suggest that I should mill my own flour. He told me that if I bought the raw grain and a hand crank machine to show support for the local farmers, then he would buy my cookies. I asked him if he had ever read Adam Smith's *The Wealth of Nations* "If I ground grain into flour," I told him, "given my current economic and time resources, I would not be able to sell my cookie bars at the given prices. I would be spending additional non-value-added hours to achieve the same end, thus losing efficiency, which translates to higher product cost." He finally understood that it is cheaper for me to buy the flour so that I can focus on baking and selling my products. "Our bakery buys most of its flour from King Arthur," I told him, "a mill in Vermont that has the best whole wheat flour in the world. They have access to the best grains and technology to achieve high levels of efficiency, making their product viable and affordable for my recipe. By turning the grinding wheel all day to get a few cups of grain, I deprive my sales effort, or even worse, my family, of much needed investments in time." Essentially, I gave him a layman's explanation on how an economy works, achieving higher productivity through interdependence.

Philosophically, our business embodies organic ideals. By working out of our home, which is state-certified for baked goods production, we use our underutilized home kitchen capacity for our business. Hence we optimize existing resources and eliminate our need to commute to another location, which substantially reduces our carbon footprint. Responding to customer feedback, I started to explore how to get the official *USDA Organic* certification. What I discovered is that it's very expensive for our home-based/start-up cookie manufacturing operation. These are the responses that I received from two organic certifiers:

CCOF - California Certified Organic Farmers

Thank you for your interest in becoming certified organic with CCOF. The process of becoming certified is fairly straightforward. To apply for certification you will need to familiarize yourself with the National Organic Program (NOP) Standards, pay a one-time $275 application fee, and submit an application. The application consists of the application form, affidavit, and Organic System Plan (OSP). The OSP is a set of forms you fill out detailing your products, facilities, and labels and how you ensure their organic integrity. After your application has been reviewed and accepted, CCOF will schedule an inspection of your facilities. Following review of the inspection report, CCOF will inform you of your certification status.

We ask that you allow about eight to twelve weeks to complete the entire process, from submitting the *application to our final certification decision. This process can often take fewer than three months, but we cannot guarantee this. (Please ask us about our expedited program, which is available for an additional fee, if you need a certification decision in fewer than eight weeks.) You can expect to pay between $1200-2000 for your first year of certification with CCOF and often less the following years as you become more familiar with the requirements, and the inspections take less time. The cost includes the one-time $275 application fee, inspection fee of $500-1000, and a minimum annual fee of $550.*

PCO – Pennsylvania Certified Organic

I received the message below from our administrative staff. From a product formulation/recipe standpoint, yes it looks like your product would be compliant with the NOP regulations. If you are interested in more information regarding the services we provide, we would be happy to send you an information package. This would contain various info about who we are, the costs and timelines involved, and many other good resources. Please note that much of this information can also be found on our website. The much-abridged version of some of the questions that you may have is:

- *You would be looking at about $1,000 total for certification fees (this includes inspection costs and assessments) your first year. This could be higher, depending on how the exact inspection fees work out.*

- *There is a cost share program which could reimburse you for up to $750.*

- *Subsequent years could be higher or lower depending on your organic sales.*

- *The first year certification cycle takes approximately 4-6 months from start to finish.*

Let me know if you'd like an information pack, and also if you have any questions. Alternatively, if you are 100% decided that you want to begin the certification process, you can order an application package via our website. If you go to our website noted below, click on Certification, then about 2/3 of the way down you'll see Download an Order Form, and print that out. Once we receive your order form along with a check for $75 (the application fee), we'll send out an application for certification packet.

We eventually found a way around the certification requirements of the above-mentioned organizations. We created an organic cashew and chocolate-chip cookie recipe that used all-certified organic ingredients. If all inputs are organic, I reasoned, then the final combined output would be organic as well. While we are not allowed to use the USDA logo, we are able to say "Made with Organic Ingredients", thus avoiding the extraordinary fees.

When we approach stores or distributors, we are always asked about shelf-life. Our cookies last about four to six weeks optimistically, since we bake without artificial preservatives. But there exists a conundrum; everyone wants their goods to be all-natural and "fresh", while at the same time they want them to last three months. What we observed is that large stores want to sell locally-made goods, but they are still bound by large corporate systems and overheads. They only take locally-made goods with long shelf lives, such as mixed nuts and barbeque sauces. The organic products that generally get shelf space are produced by large multi-national corporations.

According to Skeptoid.com, "California alone produces over $600M in organic produce, most of it coming from just five farms, who are also the same producers of most non-organic food in the state. 70 percent of all organic milk is controlled by just one major milk producer." [53] Trader Joe's is a national chain that specializes in organic, vegetarian, and alternative foods. Shoppers enjoy the image of healthful food in a small-business family atmosphere. However, Trader Joe's grossed an estimated $4.5 billion in sales (2005). The company is owned by German billionaire Theo Albrecht, ranked the 22nd richest man in the world by Forbes in 2004. He is the co-founder and CEO of German multi-national ALDI, which in 2005 had a global revenue of $37 billion. Trader Joe's increased profits by 1,000% in the 1990s, according to Business Week. Customers are willing to pay premium prices for a healthful image, but they should not delude themselves into thinking that they're supporting a local small business.

The Green Revolution

The fact is that if organic farming criteria is applied globally, it will come at the expense of virgin lands like rain forests and savannahs. Dennis Avery of the Hudson Institute's Center for Global Food Issues estimates that modern high-yield farming has saved 15 million square miles of wildlife habitat, and that if the world switched to

---

[53] Brian Dunning, Organic Food Myths, *Skeptoid.com*, January 5, 2007

organic farming, 10 million square miles of forest would need to be cut down to meet demand. [54]

Crops are threatened by insects, weather, and drought, among other things, which reduce yield per acre. Chemicals and fertilizers were introduced to protect crops from these natural inhibitors. While the world population approaches 9 billion people (by 2050), the area under cultivation remains constant. The need arises to boost crop yields on a relatively fixed supply of arable land. Genetically modified food will continue to save the world from starvation. I always tell people that we were dying in our 40s from bacteria, diarrhea, and e-coli back in the "good old days" and now we are dying of cancer in our mid 70s in the "bad new days." People need to realize that no solution is perfect and no decision is without consequences. It's a matter of weighing the pros and cons and doing a cost-benefit analysis of both.

In the mid 1960s, India was faced with very limited land resources coupled with rapid population growth. Famine was thought to be inevitable; thus, the Green Revolution took root. Started with the help of the Rockefeller Foundation, the Green Revolution was based on high-yielding varieties of wheat, rice, and other grains that had been developed in Mexico and in the Philippines.

The major benefits of the Green Revolution were experienced mainly in northern and northwestern India between 1965 and the early 1980s; the program resulted in a substantial increase in the production of food grains,

---

[54] Sarah Z. Wexler, 6 Myths About Organic Food, *Marie Claire,* March 21, 2008

mainly wheat and rice. Food-grain yields continued to increase throughout the 1980s, but the dramatic changes of the earlier years were not duplicated. By 1980, almost 75% of the total cropped area under wheat was sown with high-yielding varieties. For rice, the comparable figure was 45%. In the 1980s, the area under high-yielding varieties continued to increase, but the rate of growth overall was slower. Still, the Revolution succeeded in making high-yielding varieties available to the whole country and developing more productive strains of other crops. Moreover, higher income growth and reduced incidence of poverty were found in the states where yields increased the most.[55] To date and according to the USDA, India has not had to deal with famine since the Revolution. In fact, they are world's leading producer of coconuts, mangoes, milk, bananas, dairy products, ginger, turmeric, cashew nuts and black pepper. Furthermore, India is also the second largest producer of rice, wheat, sugar, cotton, fruits and vegetables.

However, while plants can be densely packed, livestock cannot. Regulation is needed is not needed as much in the area of grains and vegetables as it is in the production of meat and poultry products. There is a great health risk in cramming animals together into small areas and feeding them with animal byproducts. Due to meat's perishable nature, it should be locally produced.

---

[55] Wikipedia: Green Revolution in India

Greenwash

Companies are competing nowadays to demonstrate their green efforts, sometimes using them as a justification to charge us more. In reality, however, for green solutions to be acceptable, they must contribute to products that everyday people can afford. We have seen that the bio-fuels initiative led to rapid food price inflations and even starvation.[56] There needs to be an application of Six Sigma or quantitative analysis methodologies when proposing solutions, considering the whole process from supplier to end consumer. Sometimes the side-effects of the cure are greater than the problem itself.

The liberals with all their idealism need to analyze the situations holistically; otherwise their solutions will create more problems than they solve.

Political Correctness and Indecisiveness

The "how you say it is more important than what you say" pettiness is starting to infect our culture. People have to rehearse and audit every line before they speak, and they must also consider their tone and inflection so as not to offend anyone. There is nothing wrong with wanting to be polite, but perhaps we need to consider that hard data and substance is more important than tone. Moreover, political correctness is affecting our ability to work efficiently. In a lot of corporations, people are trying so hard to avoid conflict that they are sacrificing effectiveness. The people getting ahead are the ones who

---

[56] George Monbiot, The western appetite for biofuels is causing starvation in the poor world, *The Guardian*, Nov 6, 2007

fly below the radar, avoiding conflict. But it takes friction for a company to move forward, and it takes voices of opposition to make a case stronger. If everyone is agreeing all the time, how can products be improved?

While I was working at Sears, we spent an inordinate amount of time in meetings merely to gain consensus on a decision. If Sears's leadership could have been more decisive in the past decade, the company might still be the world's number one retailer. We are now becoming a nation where being ambiguity and vagueness is admired, while decisiveness labels you as a "loose cannon".

We need to get back into the habit of having vigorous and heated discussions, while relying on a leader to listen to all sides and make a final decision within pre-determined time limits.

Prefix-Americans

Placing a prefix in front of the word "American" dilutes the meaning of the word American. An American is someone who, no matter what his outward appearance, carries by birth or naturalization the ideals of our nation. Calling someone an African-American, Asian-American, or Mexican-American is counterintuitive to our goal of becoming one nation, united under liberty and with justice for all. This is Europe's big problem; they often separate people into categories based on DNA. We should not adopt this mindset. In the South, where we live now, my wife and I experience the phenomenon that people are more concerned about being polite than about being truthful. Recently, I spoke with a recruiter who finally admitted to me that I had applied for jobs for which I was not qualified. I told her that being honest with me would have allowed me to spend my energy on more relevant applications. It's better to take the bitter pill up front than to die from 1,000 polite cuts over a long period of time.

When people can express themselves in few and simple words without worrying about the consequences of offending anyone, we will start to get things done. But we are becoming a nation of disclaimers. It would make an interesting study for a Ph.D. candidate to quantify "political correctness"—the costs of speeches and legal advice

Quagmire Inc.

Quagmire Inc. depends on its boogey man, someone toward whom people can direct their fears and anger, blinding them against the facts. It is important to create a sustainable pipeline of boogey men to justify this astronomical defense budget.

Defense Spending

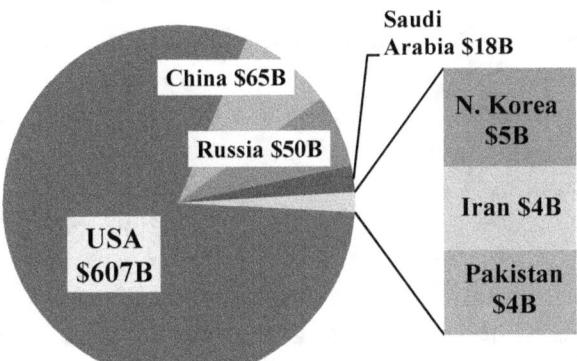

Source: Global Security.org, CIA Factbook, SIPRI

Budgets for FY 2007: Does security really have to come at the expense of our standard of living and prosperity? Or is there a better way where we can have both?

The University of Illinois at Chicago MBA offers a renowned Negotiations class that discusses distributive bargaining, setting up the grounds for negotiation and creating win-win situations. In this class, I learned about the "Power Paradox", which states that every time power is used, it is lost.

We are living in a world in which other nations and individual groups are learning to work around American imposed barriers, embargos and forceful policy, either by circumventing them through another nation (Iranians get much of what they need that is unavailable at home in Dubai) or producing the needed products at home. This is evident in the decoupling that is taking place, as predicted by Goldman Sachs several years ago; emerging economies are trading with each other to keep their economies growing, while western economies stagnate. America is entering an era where it must coexist not dominate other nations.

The past decade has been tense with our involvement in a two war predicament that just doesn't seem to end. As the military budget continues to rise[57], we need to start demanding more tangible returns from military leadership. Total world military expenditure was $1.1 Trillion (2004 est.) with the US portion being $623B (2008.)[58] or 57%. In other words, we spend more on defense than all other countries combined. Most of this rise in U.S. defense spending was due to the events of 9-11. We did need to enhance our security and intelligence capabilities to deal better with threats that use our own system against us. However, none of the objectives have been met, except removing Saddam. We need to start asking questions about how the money is being allocated. We also must ask: what does "winning" mean exactly?

---

[57] Wikipedia: Military Budget of the United States

[58] GlobalSecurity.org – Worldwide Military Expenditures data drawn from SIPRI, CIA Factbook and World Factbook.

China: Communist or Capitalist?

China is a sovereign nation with one billion people and a civilization and history as old as mankind itself. Although China's military budget is the second largest in the world, it is only around 10% of the American defense budget. Many in Washington are concerned about the double-digit increases in the Chinese military budget, which have taken place every year since 1988. However, these rises are negligible compared to U.S. defense spending. For example, 10% of $65B is $6.5B, a little less than the cost of the Joint Strike Fighter Program.[59] China is a concern which must be managed, but it is not as imminent a threat as many politicians would like us to believe. Our military budget, which outpaces China's 10 to 1, surely should accommodate any threats they may pose now or even a century down the road. What is of concern is that we are scorning a country that supports our economy. In addition to purchasing U.S. Treasuries to keep our economy liquid, China was one of the first Westinghouse AP-1000 nuclear reactor customers;   they also purchased passenger jets from Boeing and have allowed Wal-Mart, McDonald's and Cadillac to do business in their country. In fact, the Chinese are quite the capitalists themselves. Hong Kong is thriving even after the British departure, and Macau surpassed Las Vegas in gambling revenue in 2007.[60]

---

[59] Open Congressional Research Service: Defense FY 2009 Authorization and Appropriation.

[60] David Barboza, Macao Surpasses Las Vegas as Gambling Center, The New York Times, January 23, 2007

India, the world's largest democracy, has a military budget of $32B per year, and they are developing many technologies such as advanced fighters, submarines, unmanned aerial vehicles and even aircraft carriers to defend themselves against China, with whom they share a border and perceive as a threat. Moreover, the Indian armed forces stand at 1.3M active duty, the third largest fighting force in the world![61] There is a lot more to India than call centers and outsourcing, and the U.S. has a political advantage in befriending India.

What should be of concern to the US is not China's military buildup, but the fact that China is the number one holder of our debt, at $894.8 billion (in front of Japan, who holds $768.8 billion in U.S. debt instruments). Building up the military at the expense of our economy to counter China's build-up will only give the Chinese more leverage over us in the end. If Chinese investors were to start liquidating their holdings of U.S. debt, it would drastically increase the cost of borrowing for the U.S. government, as interest rates would soar. The interest bill for consumers and businesses when borrowing would also increase, crippling the fragile recovery. [62] Perhaps China will forgive our debt when we return Taiwan. We have to remember that Chinese investors are like American investors--they are free to pick and choose investments as they see fit. We are in no position to "force" anyone to buy our debt! And if we did resort to force to sell our debt, we would probably collapse anyway.

---

[61] Wikipedia: Indian Armed Forces

[62] US Treasury Department: www.ustreas.gov/tic/mfh.txt

Ultimately, the way out of our current situation is to invest in enablers for economic growth, rather than spending on security, which is far more than adequate[63].

Which is greater: Billions or Millions?

In Afghanistan, we are spending a lot of money to chase down a small group of Al-Qaeda bandits living in caves. They ride horses and use carrier pigeon as cell phones. For the amount of money we spend on the military, we should expect swift and conclusive results against such adversaries. We do have the right to question how our money is being spent when results are not being delivered.

When I presented this argument to right-wingers, they responded that "we are being forced to fight with one hand behind our back." We shouldn't have to be politically correct, they told me. "Let's kill the civilians." These are basically the same excuses we had in Vietnam. The USSR was not politically correct in their war with Afghanistan in the 1980s, and they also lost. Thus I don't find this argument valid. We can bomb both soldiers and civilians into oblivion using the Mother of All Bombs (MOAB) and Daisy Cutters, but we do not know that these enemies will submit even if we "capture the capital". These enemies are the kind who builds up enough resentment over time to keep their fire burning.

If we were to go UN-PC, targeting civilians and children, we would have a billion Muslims -- many of whom are in

---

[63] Lawrence J. Korb, Laura Conley, Sean Duggan, Slimming Down the Defense Budget, Center for American Progress, February 2, 2010

Europe, South America, Canada and even in the USA -- who are normally indifferent towards us becoming very angry all at once. This would pose some huge problems, as people living within our borders who never had any criminal past could become radicalized, overwhelming our security and leading to an economic meltdown as we continue to print money to meet budgetary shortfalls caused by excess spending responding to security threats.

The Taliban and Al Qaeda have proven themselves committed adversaries. The more we pound them, the more resilient they become. They are like us Americans— willing to take on impossible odds and incredible pain and sacrifice for what they believe. The Taliban double agent suicide attack, for example, which killed seven CIA agents on January 4, 2010 illustrates their level of commitment Taliban leaders are willing to sacrifice their own to kill high-value targets. This is not easy for western logic to comprehend.

The perception of U.S. foreign policy around the world is that Americans only help when we need something from you. Once we get it, we leave you high and dry. Indeed, we have a track record of letting down our allies: Bay of Pigs, the Kurdish uprising, and South Vietnam. While I was living in Estonia, the Russians invaded Georgia. This was of grave concern to Estonia, since their nation borders Russia, and the Russians consider Estonia one of their greatest enemies. In fact, at the Russian-Estonian border at Narva, there is a sign on the Russian side going into Estonia that says, "You are now entering a fascist nation". My Estonian colleagues thought the Americans were going to stand by Georgia, the fledgling democracy, in accordance with NATO Article 5. To their disappointment, the American response consisted of Condoleezza Rice wrote a letter to Russia that ultimately was nothing more than a slap on the wrist. Most nations in the world, with the exception of the Baltics, figured out our foreign policy long ago when it comes to looking out for nations with no resources.

After the Americans achieved their objective of driving out the Soviets from Afghanistan in the 1980s, Pakistan was left high and dry. As soon as the Russians left, so did our commitment, advisors and money, leaving Pakistan with a refugee crisis, a flood of Kalashnikov rifles (AK-47's) and extremists who put their nation on the brink of a political and economic crisis. The Pakistani intelligence service known as the ISI worked with Afghan mullahs known as the Taliban to help create a Sharia nation which would contain the radicals. General Pervez Musharraf, the President of Pakistan at the time of 9-11, stated in his speech to the UN just after the attacks that he would not allow Pakistan to be let down again.

The American leadership is delusional to think that some goat herder will turn in Osama Bin Laden (OBL). First, the goat herder would have to find him and want to turn him in. Second, the goat herder would have to find American troops or relay this information to a higher-up, who would probably kill him for betraying his people. Third, even if the goat herder succeeded, there would be reprisals on his family and relatives. If OBL is ever going to be caught, it will be at the highest levels of tribal council or government, the same ones with whom we are working. Ironically, our taxpayers indirectly pay the Taliban through private security firms, who protect our resupply convoys while passing through tribal regions of

Afghanistan. These firms pay off militia leaders who control key stretches of road, many of whom are loyal to the Taliban.[64]

A person like OBL needs state support to remain hidden for so long. I am not into conspiracy theories, and I do believe our forces are doing their best to find him, but I am also a firm believer in mathematics and logic. In my opinion, the reason we haven't caught OBL is a matter of basic finance. Just after 9-11, the US gave Pakistan $12B for their help in supporting our efforts with the War on Terror. Between 2002 and 2008, we gave Pakistan$6.6B in direct aid to support their military[65]. In 2009, a bill was passed to offer Pakistan $7.5B in non-military aid over the next five years.[66] This totals $26.1B, or about $2B per year over 14 years (2001 to 2014). The bounty for OBL's head is $50M. We have to bear in mind that Pakistanis are quite good in math and business. Why would you sell your goose who lays $2B annually in golden eggs for a one-time $50M? The GAO in a 2008 report suggests that the Pakistani government overbilled the U.S. government for military operations, and the Defense Department paid out billions in reimbursement claims without proper

---

[64] Aram Roston, How the US Funds the Taliban, *The Nation*, November 11, 2009

[65] Nathan Hodge, Surprise! Pakistan Siphoned off Billions in U.S. Military Aid, *Wired Magazine*, October 5, 2009

[66] Derrick Z. Jackson, US Aid to Pakistan a Shell Game, *The Boston Globe*, October 6, 2009

documentation. [67] Essentially OBL will be turned over when it makes good business sense for the Pakistani government to do so, not anytime sooner. The basis of our strategy should be to make it worthwhile for Pakistan to turn him in, instead of our wasting billions year after year.

Which is greater: $85 or $29?

Prior to the Iraq war in 2003, oil was at $29 per barrel. Now in 2010, oil prices are expected to hover around $70-$85 per barrel. Secretary of Defense Donald Rumsfeld and then-Director of the Office of Management and Budget Mitchell Daniels estimated the likely costs of the Iraq war to be between $50 billion to $60 billion. Paul Wolfowitz, then-Undersecretary of Defense (now president of the World Bank Group) asserted that increased Iraqi oil revenues would pay for the war. When Lawrence Lindsey, then-Presidential Economic Adviser, suggested that the actual costs may be closer to $100 billion or even $200 billion, the White House called those figures grossly exaggerated and swiftly showed him to the door. [68] Now we see that Lindsey's figures grossly underestimated the costs, which were in actually ten times higher.

We went into Iraq on the premise of "imminent threat" of WMD attack, only to find out that we had faulty

---

[67] Nathan Hodge, Surprise! Pakistan Siphoned off Billions in U.S. Military Aid, *Wired Magazine*, October 5, 2009

[68] Craig Lambert, Iraq Black Hole – The $2 Trillion War, *Harvard Magazine*, May-June 2006

intelligence. The government quickly tried to find other reasons for the invasion. Gordon Brown, the current British PM and former leader of the Labour Party, stated that he went to war because "Iraq breached international obligations"[69]. Their American counterparts tried to make a link between Saddam Hussein and Bin Laden, which was ludicrous. That was about as likely as Hugh Heffner and Pat Robertson meeting up for golf. Bin Laden is a "true believer" who left behind earthly possessions for an idealistic quest. Bin Laden believed Saddam Hussein was an infidel.[70]

This made sense. Although Saddam's Iraq was a dictatorship, the society was mostly secular; women had jobs and held cabinet positions. Saddam went from rags to riches and led a decadent life: castles, sports cars, expensive clothes. Bin Laden, on the other hand, went from castles to caves when he declared jihad in Afghanistan. As I recall, when Iraq invaded Kuwait in 1991, Bin Laden offered the services of his experienced mujahedeen warriors to oust Saddam's Republican Guard. Instead, the Saudis turned to the Americans, which fueled his anger toward the West.

It amazes me how we were manipulated as a nation by White House and military leadership into entering this debacle. The basis for war was clearly emotional. Our allies warned us against it, as did the UN and every other

---

[69] BBC, WMD not reason I backed Iraq war, says Gordon Brown, February 19, 2010.

[70] Samia Nakhoul, Bin Laden Labels Saddam an Infidel, *Reuters*, February, 11, 2003

rational American leader. Iraqi Freedom has cost our country around $2 trillion, not only in war-related expenditures (including long-term care of wounded soldiers) but also in the cost of inflation related to prolonged elevated oil prices.[71] Bear in mind that a trillion is a million-million, or one thousand billion.

It would have been better and most likely cheaper, to work out a deal with Saddam Hussein to take refugees, the misfits from their society, and offer them asylum in America and other western nations. There are many places in Saskatchewan[72] and the rural USA such as North Dakota in dire need of people.[73] I am certain it would have been cheaper to get them started in farming or services than to invest so much into "nation building." Moreover, the money spent on repatriating refugees to the USA would have found its way into the domestic economy. We have taken refugee immigrants in the past, i.e., the Ellis Island days, with great success. I have personally seen Somali refugees become millionaire business owners while creating jobs in the USA..

Hercules and Antaeus

Iran has been a grave concern to the U.S. recently because of their nuclear weapons ambitions. Senator Bob Kerry

---

[71] Craig Lambert, Iraq Black Hole – The $2 Trillion War, *Harvard Magazine*, May-June 2006

[72] The Leader-Post (Regina), Immigration logjam makes labour shortage worse, *Working.com*, February 8, 2008

[73] Kathy Kiely, Can aging N.D. resist change amid immigration debate?, *USA Today,* November 26, 2007

stated that he believed Iran has been the greatest threat all along during his 2004 presidential campaign.

In considering the current conundrum with Iran and the war on terror, I am reminded of Greek mythology. Antaeus, the son of Gaia and Poseidon, was a Libyan giant whose immense strength appeared invincible. He challenged all travelers to a wrestling match, which he invariably won. Upon winning, he slaughtered his adversaries and collected their skulls so that one day he could build a temple to his father- Poseidon, the Greek god of the sea.

Hercules was on his way back from the Hesperides when the giant challenged him to a wrestling match. He was indefatigably strong, as long as he remained in contact with the earth (his mother), but once lifted into the air he became as weak as other men. Hercules, finding that he could not beat Antaeus by throwing him to the ground, where he would regain his strength, soon discovered the secret of his power. Holding Antaeus aloft, Hercules crushed him to death in a bear hug. I believe there are parallels between this myth and our current strategy in the Middle East. The more we try to punish Iran and threaten them with military action, the stronger and more unified they become. Instead, we must separate them from their source of power: the high value of oil.

The U.S. military is the world's largest consumer of oil in the world. We consume 144 million barrels per year and 395, 000 barrels per day in 2004.[74] This is around 40

---

[74] US Defense Energy Support Center Fact Book 2004

million barrels per year more than we used in peacetime. Thus, Iran has benefited the most from our Iraqi adventure, with its GDP rising from $135B in 2003 to $385B in 2008, resulting in 185% growth.[75] American forces helped relieve Iran's Western border of a longtime adversary (Saddam Hussein), while the conflict helped push oil prices up, thus fueling Iran's economic boom, which is mostly based on oil production.

GDP of Iran ($ billions)

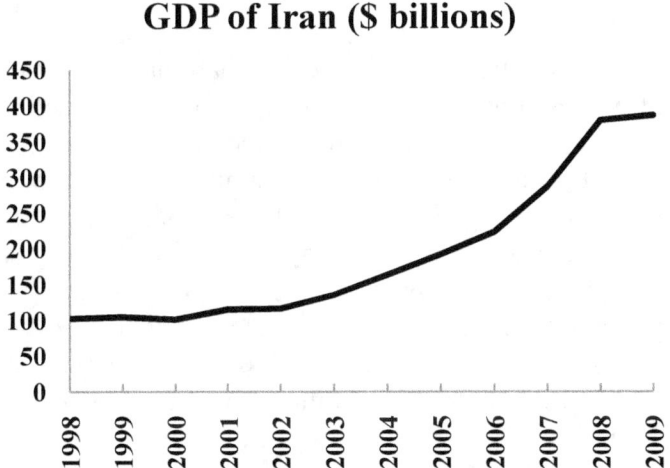

Although we embargo Iran, we continue to buy oil from them indirectly. The oil market works as anonymous producers pumping oil into a giant tub, and buyers dip their cups in the tub after paying the market price set on one of the global exchanges. Not only do supply and demand fundamentals affect oil prices, but so do war and speculation about global uncertainty. These factors add

---

[75] World Bank Data Finder

premium to the oil prices as well. In other words, it's pretty hard to punish Iran. The more we threaten them, the more money they get. Moreover, the Bush's administration's success with the go-it-alone policy in Iraq managed to get us zero support from our NATO and Middle Eastern Allies to counter the Iranian nuclear threat. The misguided invasion into Iraq gave Iran justification to build up their military on the grounds that they could face an unprovoked attack from the Bush Administration.

With this newfound wealth, the international community was unwilling to back the Americans and lowered defense expenditures associated with protecting their western border with Iraq, Iran embarked on a nuclear program and put a satellite in space, making them potentially able to send a nuclear warhead anywhere in the world. Additionally, the Iranians covertly funded pro-Shia groups in Iraq to keep the Americans bogged down.[76] Seemingly everyone in the world currently trades with Iran except the Americans. China, Germany, Japan, Italy, and France have trade programs with Iran. In Tehran, one can buy Toyotas, Mercedes Benzes, laptop computers and even designer western clothes. Perhaps this prosperity will be the Mullah's undoing, just as Glasnost was the undoing of the USSR. A majority of Iran's population is under 25 and not very enthusiastic about the revolution; however, they would fight against an American invasion.

---

[76] John J. Kruzel, Iran Continues to Subvert Iraq, Officials Say, *American Forces Press Service*, February 17, 2010

While Iran prospers from the results of the American invasion, the average American has not seen any tangible benefit from the Iraq war; in fact we are worse off now than we were in 2003. Moreover, the number of civilian casualties in Iraq has probably fueled more anger towards us, thus creating more terrorists down the line. I am glad that there was a change of guard so that at the very least we don't get ourselves into a new quagmire.

The way to win this war is through economics; we must render oil insignificant and worthless by developing new technology (discussed in Section III).

Terror Economics

Al-Qaeda has a cut and dry objective—to destroy the West and those who oppose Al-Qaeda's radical views. They have been active not only in America and Europe but also in India, Indonesia and the Middle East. Although this group is radical in nature, they have mastered the art of manipulating our system against us; much like a Judo athlete uses his opponent's strength and momentum to his advantage. Unlike white supremacist radical groups in the United States, the higher-ups in Al-Qaeda are well-educated, patient and adaptive. Bin Laden himself attended King Abd Al Aziz University in Jeddah, Saudi Arabia, where he studied civil engineering, business administration, economics and public administration. Instead of pursuing a career in community economic development, however, Bin Laden used his combined background in politics, economics and engineering to gain an all encompassing understanding of modern warfare (both technical and economic). Understanding his background helps us understand how he fights against us.

US National Debt

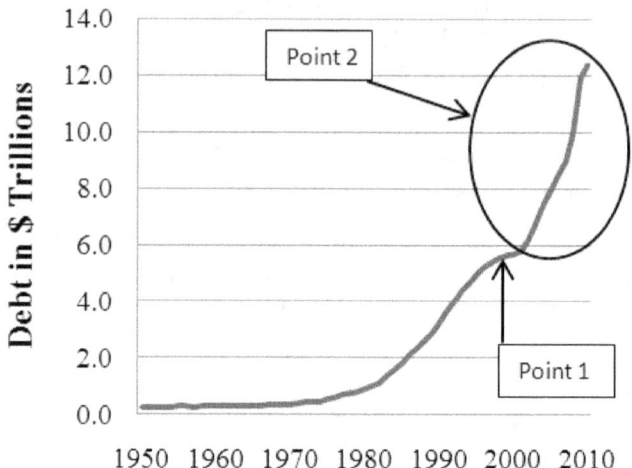

Source: US Treasury

Point 1: Prior to the War on Terror, our deficit was just starting to level off. During these days, the dollar was as strong as $.86 = 1 euro.

Point 2: Since the wars in Iraq and Afghanistan, our deficit has skyrocketed while our economic growth has slowed to a halt. *Terror Economics* aims to increase debt while subduing economic growth in an effort to bust our economy. Thus, it's wise for the enemy to maintain low-intensity conflict in an effort to divert our resources from investment at home to expense abroad.

Anyone who is hell bent on destroying America has figured out that it would be impossible to conduct a full frontal military assault. Instead, their aim is to harass our emergency and security services in order to provoke a response that requires heavy spending on our part. Every time we respond to a false alarm, it costs our enemies much less than it costs us to respond.

Moreover, there are massive amounts of lost productivity associated with security alerts and shutdowns. Eventually the money spent on security has to be made up somewhere else. We can raise taxes, cut services or borrow to get the extra money needed to cover the shortfall.

9-11 was a diversion, not the main attack. OBL expected a forceful military response. His goal was to divert our resources from domestic investment in infrastructure, which enables future growth, to external war expenditure, which has no return.

Winning for OBL means keeping the war going in an effort to drain our economy. Neither Afghanistan nor Iraq has given us any return on the blood or treasure invested. Thus, such responses have to be measured with clear objectives, contingencies and exits. Perhaps this sounds like admitting defeat; however, if we keep dancing to their tunes, we will surely lose.

Ironically, the more we fight these wars, the more speculative uncertainty is created in the oil markets, pushing the prices higher. Ultimately, they see an increase in funding. Al-Qaeda doesn't own any oil wells, but I am sure their benefactors and supporters who have E-trade accounts and trade USO or UCO oil Electronically Traded Funds (ETFs) would be upset if oil prices were to fall sharply.

At some point, if we keep diverting more resources abroad at a greater rate than what we take in, our treasury will bust and we will be unable to fight altogether. The results of ensuing high rates of unemployment, coupled with a declining currency, will trigger an increase in crime and strain public services, further draining the economy's output. This form of warfare is neither as visible nor as glamorous, but it is far more effective than using troops, tanks and planes. Moreover, this prolonged heightened state of alert creates anxiety within our society, making us impotent as a nation. Terrorism is an affordable option for those who do not possess the military might to take on the greatest fighting force the planet has ever seen.

Parallel examples:

- During World War II, we devoted tremendous resources to crippling the German economy, sending B-17s to bomb factories throughout Europe. This made it more difficult for them to wage war. The terrorists are using the same indirect approach by keeping us on an extended mission that, over the long haul, erodes our economy, which in turn limits our ability to wage war. The terrorists aim is to collapse "The Great Satan" under the weight of its own sword. The more time passes, the more difficult it is to hold up the sword. We increase our defense spending at the expense of infrastructure and education, crippling our ability to grow the economy while the costs of the war become more expensive.

- During the Civil War, the Union used a Naval Blockade against the South. The strategy, part of the Anaconda Plan of General Winfield Scott, required the closure of 3,500 miles of Confederate coastline and twelve major ports, including New Orleans, Louisiana, and Mobile, Alabama, the top two cotton-exporting ports prior to the outbreak of the War. As a result, Confederate cotton exports were reduced 95%

during the blockade period. By creating red alerts and forcing us to divert resources, the terrorists are blockading our ability to innovate and grow our economy.

Basically, the terrorists just have to create the perception that danger exists. Public resource expenditures are cut to pay for defense spending. Currently, many communities around the nation are using Federal stimulus money to cover budget shortfalls.[77] Stimulus money only delays the inevitable; eventually the "free money" will be gone.

Terrorists don't work for free. They need to secure their families and financial futures. They need transportation, lodging and clothing like everyone else. Terror groups, like any other group, raise funds, most of which comes from state sponsors like Iran, or wealthy individuals connected to oil. This war can go two ways; we can cripple them financially by focusing our war effort on an economic versus a military response, or we can continue to pursue a policy of insanity, where we do the same thing over and over but expect a different result, bankrupting ourselves in the process.

Citizen Counterterrorism

The terrorists are transforming our society from an open and free one built on innovation to a state-controlled society dependent on government spending. How do we win against this? The answer lies in being self-reliant.

---

[77] Michael Gormley, US Federal Stimulus Money to Avoid School Layoffs Will Leave Budget Shortfalls, Associated Press, December 21, 2009

There is only so much security we can afford before it cripples our production capacity. When on flights, we must take notice of those around us, engage in conversations and keep our eyes open. In our neighborhoods and communities, we need to reach out and befriend lonely and isolated people. The biographies of terrorists reveal that many of their personal issues are rooted in isolation, humiliation and loneliness. Perhaps when a potential terrorist makes some local friends, he may instead become an asset on his own accord.

Simply being nice to strangers and people different from us could probably save billions of dollars. This may sound unbelievably simplistic, but the path to jihad begins like this: A young man from a conservative family shows promise of becoming a doctor or engineer. In his native country, he is highly revered and respected, but his intellect easily exhausts the educational resources of his home nation. Most Middle Eastern families and youth believe, rightfully so, that the best education in science and medicine is in the West, in America and Europe. A Western education is prestigious. In many instances, an entire extended family will exhaust their financial resources to send a single son or daughter abroad to study. Generally, The United States is the preferred destination, as the schools are considered to be more innovative and cutting-edge, and the society more accepting of immigrants. However, those who do not qualify or cannot afford U.S. schools generally go to Western Europe to further their studies. Upon arrival in Europe or America, the immigrant enters a state of culture shock, going through a series of emotional and logistical adjustments.

Western Europeans often believe that immigrants who enter their country to study or work should adopt their culture. Many Middle Eastern immigrants to Europe hold high-value jobs in engineering and medicine and pay taxes to the society, yet they and even their children are stigmatized as outsiders. When I was living in Sweden, I befriended a Swedish man of Turkish origin who was a locomotive engineer/driver. I commented that it must be nice to be Swedish; he quickly corrected me, saying that he will never be Swedish, even though he was born and raised in Sweden. He even served in the Swedish army and spoke the language fluently. He explained that you have to be Swedish in looks and genetics; the nationality can't be adopted like an American identity can be adopted in the U.S.. America's unique ability to assimilate people comes from a legacy of its being a meritocracy: in general, Americans will tolerate those different than themselves if the nation can better achieve their overall goals with immigrants' participation.

In the past, immigrants arrived with families, often already married, thus having an emotional cushion against the shocks associated with moving to a new country. Lately, the trend is that the young men are entering Western nations as singles, having greater need for comfort and a sense of identity. In my experiences living in Europe, most of the young Middle Eastern males come to Europe with a sense of enthusiasm that they will be living in a free and modern society. However, as time passes and the realities of everyday life set in, these males start to feel isolated and withdrawn from society. They yearn to find someone who understands them. Under normal circumstances, most of these educated émigrés resent fundamentalists and extremists as undereducated hindrances to progress. But sometimes the fundamentalists are the only ones offering friendship. I can speak from my personal experiences that Middle Easterners, Indians and Pakistanis are highly sociable and gregarious people who enjoy being around large groups of people, mainly family and friends.

Feelings of isolation can lead to resentment against the host nation. Within the Mosques and other ethnic organizations sometimes reside radical elements, who offer to fill these voids. As the immigrants become more involved with these groups, they have less time and desire to integrate into the mainstream of society. I always found that highly intelligent pissed-off people are the most dangerous. At the same time, I find highly intelligent happy people to be the most generous and kind.

I never felt "Indian" until I started to live and work in a full-time civilian job in the American South. After talking to locals who think India is made up only of slums and call centers, I felt this burning nationalism for India, a nation I visited often but never lived in.

When I was young, I wanted to distance myself from being Indian as much as possible; when I visited India, I wanted to leave as quickly as I arrived. But after a dose of prolonged Southern living, I can understand what a young intelligent male émigré from the Middle East feels when he is here. Misery combined with isolation rarely leads to anything good.

One day, while I was having a conversation with my colleague's wife, I brought up the fact that some of my female cousins had arranged marriages. She told me that someone in her church was divorcing from one, and she could never imagine having an arrange marriage herself. Although I told her that this is the norm for most of the world (India, Asia, the Middle East and Africa). Western marriages (5% divorce rate for arranged marriages, while Western marriages divorce around 50% of the time[78]) she gave me a look that said she still thought Westerns were far superior. Much of the world sees Western culture as highly hypocritical; we allow our daughters to party like crazy over spring break, attend college and graduates school as single women, but expect them to marry as virgins at the age of 27. My friends abroad always comment how Americans eat Big Macs but then drink diet soda.

Europeans tend to have a similar arrogance toward family and marriage; they believe marriage is for uneducated people. Consequently, Europe is suffering from low birthrates, which is leading to depopulation.[79] In a time that demands more mutual understanding, and with a critical-skills labor shortage looming, many European politicians are running on a nationalist agenda, which advocates that immigrants should assimilate to European culture. It is ironic that true Europeans are not replenishing themselves and yet they expect the immigrants and their children, who will carry their economy in the future, to adopt a mentality that leads to

---

[78] Nisha Danny, The Reality of Arranged Marriages, *Helium.com*

[79] Paul S. Hewitt, Depopulation and Ageing in Europe and Japan: The Hazardous Transition to a Labor Shortage Economy, *International Politics and Society*, January 2002

extinction. The Swiss have banned minarets[80] and many of the European nations are introducing laws to ban headscarves. To an American, this is appalling

It is not enough to just offer immigrants schooling and a job. We as Americans, if we want to counter terrorism in a cost effective manner that doesn't compromise our own personal freedom, must also offer a genuine hand of friendship with no strings attached. Since we arrived in the South, the only offers of friendship my wife and I have received has been an invitation to join a mega-church and MLM's. It's time we ask foreigners instead how they do things back home, what they eat and what they find fulfilling. Perhaps we will find that kebab and rice is healthier than hotdogs and potato chips. Our nation became great by taking the best traditions from around the world and integrating them into our own. We have to make an effort to reach out to strangers and include them, and perhaps their values, in the fabric of our communities. After reaching out and making extra effort to be inclusive, the new arrivals will more than likely see us fellow human beings instead of as "infidels" and more than likely see that pursuing financial and intellectual endeavors is more rewarding than pursuing destructive ones. This may sound like an extremely liberal approach; however, from a cost angle, this is a far cheaper solution than setting up security and surveillance systems.

---

[80] Alexander G. Higgins, 57% of Swiss Vote to Ban Minarets, AP, November 30, 2009

Who Profits From The Cyclical Madness?

Quagmire is big business, and many people want it to continue. The sales of war-related products and services bring in tremendous profit with little competition. The amount of money we devote to defense spending has helped an entire industry thrive (KBR, Halliburton, General Dynamics, and Blackwater), has even creating some billionaires, while the nation's economy has downshifted from steady growth to near-depression. Applying logic, one can see it would be in the defense industry's best interest to sustain and continue conflict. Peace and stability threaten the bottom line..[81]

What we have now is a leadership crisis of epic proportions. In this case, the leaders are generals and admirals, the executives of the military. Traditionally, the finest career officers are groomed for these "flag officer" positions when they are Commanders/Lt. Colonels. They are sent to the War College and to further their study of history and global affairs. Many flag officers have become great presidents: General George Washington, General Ulysses Grant and General Dwight Eisenhower, to name a few. Many others have become corporate executives in Fortune 50 firms.

I often hear grumblings that the military would be better off if it weren't for the politicians. However, if that were the case, we would be living in the former USSR or in North Korea. It is effective for military leadership to

---

[81] Michael Brush, Who's profiting from the Iraq war?, MSN, August 27, 2007.

serve under civilian leadership, and we must work within those constraints. This is the American way.

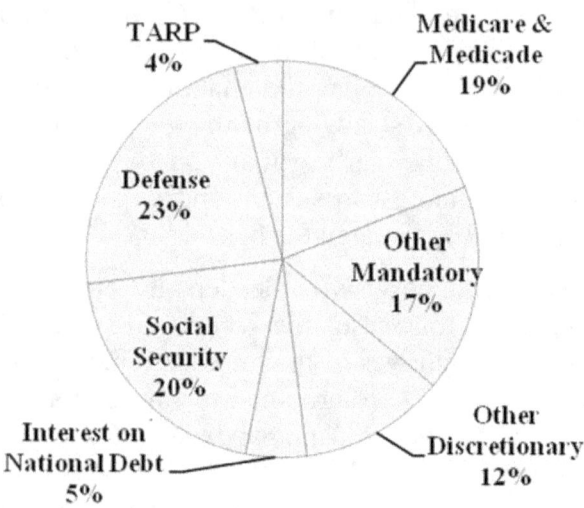

US Federal Spending -
FY 2009 ($ Billion) Total $3.518 Trillion

Source: Whitehouse Office of Management & Budget

This means that flag officers are not only in charge of managing the military; they are also stewards of our nation's economy. When they make decisions, they must consider not only the cost of lives and munitions, but also the effect on the long-term health of our nation's economy. Killing pirates who impede commerce, for example, ultimately benefits our economy. Offensive war is a means of last resort to ensure that our nation's economy continues to prosper. We must also use diplomacy as a force multiplier, leveraging our allies to help achieve our greater objectives, while limiting the impact to our economy.

The first Desert Storm war was a prime example of this policy. We managed to contain Saddam Hussein with full allied support and, best of all, our allies paid for it. In fact, our nation ran a surplus. In essence, we got in, got out and got paid. Saddam was kept in his box.[82] In some cases we must intervene to protect the defenseless, as in Kosovo or Liberia. However, this must be done in a well-planned and measured manner with clear timelines, objectives and exits based on financial and time limits; otherwise we could fall into a quagmire, spending ourselves into oblivion.

Recently, I have not seen a flag officer let alone any military leader talk publically in a forthright manner about how the wars are impacting our overall economy. Flag officers are not only selected for their stellar performance, but also for a love of country, so strong that they are not afraid to say, "We need to use something other than military force to win." The terrorist attacks of 9-11 killed almost 3,500 people. The cost to rebuild the trade centers will range from $4-12 billion.[83] The response to 9-11 cost our nation around 6,500 lives (troops, contractors and journalists), almost 50,000 seriously injured troops and contractors, and almost a trillion dollars.[84] I am not sure what the definition of a win is, but this does not seem to be it. Already, we are printing money to keep our

---

[82] AP, US May Profit if Allies Pay Their War Pledges, *Rome News Tribune,* March 26, 1991

[83] MSNBC, New Trade Center tower design unveiled, December 20, 2003.

[84] UnknownNews.net and the Associated Press

economy moving. If we lose our AAA sovereign rating, other nations will be less inclined to buy our debt.[85]

Our current flag officers need to take more classes in economics and finance, and also intern in the private sector, so that they can be exposed to non-military perspectives as well. They need to implement "stop-losses" so that we exit a quagmire the same way a company exits a bad investment decision -- immediately. Right now most generals and admirals use the term "stop-loss" to keep people in the military beyond their initial commitment.

Hence, before committing resources, which include human lives and public monies, there needs to be a business plan conveying what we hope to achieve, how much it will cost, the possible financial benefits and the exit strategies. For example, it is quite clear that attacking pirates on the high seas has a clear exit strategy, will ensure that more cargo travels safely, eases fears about shipping cargo being lost, and lowering consumer prices.

The Generals and Admirals are supposed to be the link between the needs of the U.S. Economy and the capabilities of the U.S. Military What we see instead are flag officers who are getting paid $100K - $200K per year on active duty and around $100K per year in retirement, as they are hired by defense contractor firms as board members. Many retired flag officers, while they work for the defense industry, are also retained by the military as "mentors" while being compensated at rates of around

---

[85] Ambrose Evans-Pritchard, China warns Federal Reserve over 'printing money', *Telegraph (UK)*, May 24, 2009.

$200-$340 per hour. [86] Although they are required to "sit out" one year after retiring before joining the defense sector, they are still sought for their connections.

Much of this problem is rooted in the government culture of waste. Bureaucrats and military leaders are given budgets every year, and they want to spend this money as quickly as possible to ensure they get at least the same amount or more next year. After years and years of doing this, they believe in their minds that this practice is okay and even commendable.

When I was in the Navy, I heard stories about how excess fuel was being dumped overboard prior to returning to port so that the skipper could ensure he would get at least the same amount of fuel, if not more, the following year. When I was transitioning out of the military and into the private sector, the corporate recruiter told us that doing this in the private sector would surely get you fired.

The military is an excellent organization which has trained and provided skilled labor and leaders to American industry. The GI Bill has been a win-win for both soldiers and American corporations. However, we must manage this organization wisely so that it continues to help the nation, not impede or reverse progress.

There are no absolutes. Using history as a guide without considering current events is reckless. For instance, believing that liberating Iraq and Afghanistan would be

---

[86] Tom Vanden Brook, Ken Dilanian and Ray Locker, Retired military officers cash in as well-paid consultants, *USA Today*, November 18, 2009

similar to liberating Germany got us into a big mess. What worked in the past may not work in the future as warfare evolves. Warfare in the beginning was just weapons and soldiers on a battlefield; now it is has an economic, political and cultural dimension.

The Bottom Line

Parties today seem more interested in grabbing headlines than in looking at the cold, hard facts. Corporations and the media exploit our trust by playing on our emotions.

We need to focus on the key issues that really matter, ones that are visible, quantifiable and, when fixed, create lasting solutions. We need to look at data in a cold, financial and decisive manner and allocate public money using economics, not emotions or tradition.

Real solutions do not sell coffee cups, conventions, t-shirts and bumper stickers. Detailed plans and projects that include project cost estimates, alternatives, timelines, expected returns on investment and spin-off effects are too boring for the media. This means we have a lot of hard work ahead of us as citizens.

Criticizing our own country is not the same as hating our country. In fact, it's the greatest expression of love. Kids raised by flattering and apologetic parents grow up without the proper skills to make it on their own in society. Relying on the nation to fix itself is as ludicrous an idea as relying on a teenager with a substance-abuse problem to voluntarily check himself into rehab.

People are screaming, but they have no idea what they are screaming for. Instead of fighting for causes, many people these days are fighting for the sake of fighting. We need to get off our sofas and start becoming citizens. Democracy is only as effective as its participants. We the people must do work within the system to vote, advocate, and write to our Congressmen. Our system has plenty of means by which we can make effective change. We just need to start using them.

PART III –STIMULUS

Leaders vs. Politicians

We suffer from a leadership crisis. Bureaucrats often look out for their own benefit before the nation's, and most working men and women are doing the same. People are afraid that if they make a mistake then they can lose their job, precipitating survival mode behavior. People are afraid to disagree, even when it may be the right thing to do. We have seen the results of this broken culture manifest itself in tragedy at NASA,[87] various security breaches and the miscalculations in Iraq and Afghanistan.

Those currently on the sidelines with the power of celebrity, wealth and affluence should be expected to step up into leadership roles.

But while politicians and those in power are partially at fault for our nation's decline, the American people are also guilty. We let ourselves be manipulated by clever ads and bright colors. We don't research or question the information we are given; we just accept it.

We need to elect leaders who are willing to make unpopular short-term decisions for the long-term greater good. These leaders need to explain to their constituents the cost-benefit analysis of the sacrifices we will be asked to make.

Leaders must be visionaries. In essence, national leaders must be a combination of both pragmatists and dreamers. When James Monroe stated his doctrine of Manifest

---

[87] James Oberg, NASA's Culture of Denial, *NBC News*, August 25, 2003

Destiny, there was no way to determine all the costs or benefits, but people knew that a nation spanning two oceans would be nothing short of magnificent. Almost two hundred years later, it's still hard to comprehend the benefits of reaching our destiny. Similarly, today's leaders need to focus on one or two major themes, maintaining our nation's unprecedented ascent through history. And we should elect those in favor of term limits. Turnover in government may turn politicians into leaders once they realize they can't make a career on the public dole; the elected official may be more inclined to make a contribution to the nation and his legacy instead being pre-occupied with campaigns and fiefdom building.

Term limits will help stamp out this "I've been here longer, so I'm always right" mentality. Moreover, when a few of these career bureaucrats work together for long periods of time, a group think starts to form and newcomers cannot effectively express their ideas.

We need people who are willing to move mountains, like New York Governor DeWitt Clinton did in 1817 when he secured funding for the Erie Canal. Good leadership has a lot in common with good parenting. If we feed children only what they want when they are young, they will grow up overweight and spoiled, with social and physical problems that hinder their performance in society. Parents who exercise leadership will feed their kids fruits and vegetables, restrict junk food and impose some outdoor time. The parents will keep their kids within clearly defined boundaries. The child may resent the parents during growth, but when he graduates from Harvard he will thank his parents in his commencement address. Leaders must guide their people through the short-term sacrifices required to attain the long-term, sustainable prosperity that has been the cornerstone of American culture.

Leaders know when their time is up. George Washington voluntarily stepped down after two terms and in doing so set a precedent that should be followed by all politicians. Term limits allow for a constant flow of new ideas and visions. And we need to actively advocate this kind of government, since we the people are the government!

Stimulating Numbers

Our government workers are mostly sitting behind desks doing studies that give reasons why we can't do things, instead of getting out there and doing meaningful work. Thus, when stimulus money runs out, we will only have a lot of paperwork to show for all this borrowing against our future.

Statistical Stimulus

Economic Headlines

Temporary Caulking Jobs

Need for New Stimulus

Tax Money　　　**"Green Bureaucracy Job Growth"**　　　**Economic Benefit**

Statistical Stimulus is based on the principle of spending taxpayer money to create new bureaucracies. Career bureaucrats micromanage a lot of small projects, which in turn stimulates economic indicator numbers that lure speculators back into the market, re-inflating the bubble economy.

Headlines today say things are getting better, but no one is asking how this happened. If you print trillions of dollars and spend it on small "shovel ready" projects, of course it will catalyze the economy and create some kinetic energy. However, we must ask, "What happens after the Stimulus?"

161

While at Sears Product Repair Services, I learned about the balanced score card, which put into place measures that gauged the effectiveness of the service technicians. They were rated on such metrics as completes per day, cost per repair and trips per repair, with one metric being the focus. Based on the key metric, the technicians were able to meet their goal. However, the other metrics would suffer. When management wanted completes per day maximized, the technicians would rush through jobs to hit their targets. However, the trips per repair number would then rise, as technicians who were rushing while performing diagnostics were unable to render an accurate first-time solution. Thus, the service technician would meet his goals, but the customer would suffer, along with Sears, which had to take losses from multiple attempts to fix the same problem.

"Hitting numbers" is part of the American corporate culture. While this works in some cases, building a nation is a multi-dimensional project, and it is important to make sure that overall goals are being met. While it may work in fast food or retail management, it doesn't work in health care, energy or national security.

The current stimulus only aims to hit a number—jobs created or saved by a certain date. However, it does nothing to address the issue of what happens when the money runs out, like effects on our currency. The bailout and subsequent stimulus was necessary, according to leading economists worldwide. Without it we would have had a sudden crash instead of a controlled hard landing.[88] In our darkest hours, we were given a great opportunity to re-invent our nation, which our leaders should have seized upon. Instead, we had politicians trying to grab small chunks of stimulus money to help their campaign financiers.

I personally witnessed this parasitic mentality when I attended a Federal Green Jobs Legislative Conference. Sponsored by the Green Jobs Alliance, the conference was comprised of construction trade companies, community organizations and the local AFL-CIO. On the panel, experts described how communities can divide the stimulus funds originating from our tax money. Moreover, the contractors were able to use the conference to get green certifications, which they could use as a marketing tool. The conference also discussed tax incentives. I have learned, however, that in many cases these incentives don't give us back as much money as we actually believe. Most incentives allow us to deduct the amount of the incentive off our taxable income, not the actual amount of the project from the taxes we pay. Moreover, it takes a significant number of jobs in middle management within state and local agencies just to manage the processing of these programs. Energy conservation has been around for as long as I can remember. When I was a kid my father bought 3M cellophane window wraps every winter, which were inflated with a hairdryer to prevent cold air from coming

---

[88] Steven Mufson and Lori Montgomery, Economists Agree Time Is of the Essence for Stimulus, *The Washington Post*, February 8, 2009

into the house. I remember installing Owens's Corning insulation in the attic and changing shower heads to reduce water usage as well. What I found perplexing about all this green-hype is that there is nothing new about the fact that if you spend money on insulation, caulk, new windows and more efficient appliances, your energy bills will decline. However, the government has decided to call common sense conservation "going green," resulting in new bureaucratic layers tasked with micromanaging a complex system of grants, audits, rules and regulations to monitor window caulking. This is better known as "Cash for Caulkers." The HOMESTAR program requires, for example, that before we insulate our homes, we must contact an energy auditor prior, hire a certified contractor and then submit a lot of paperwork, merely to get this tax break or a rebate.[89] This process has a lot of moving parts, which require oxygen, offices, pens, computers and federal employees, among other things.

At the conference, the National Manager for the EPA's (Environmental Protection Agency) Energy Star program told the audience, "The money passes through many sieves, where it's reduced at each point, before reaching you." Basically, he was admitting that there are a lot of government overheads absorbing funds meant for energy conservation. Much of those funds pay for overhead—the salaries, stimulus money managers, accountants, office

---

[89] Bill Schmick, Cash for Caulkers – A No Brainer for Consumers, *A Few Dollars More*, March 4, 2010.

furniture, and energy bills—instead of their intended purpose.

I am a firm believer that a society needs taxes in order to develop and become more efficient. In fact, there is nothing wrong with taxes. What's wrong is the management of tax revenue. When the government directs resources to windows and caulk, it will create more jobs and boost that sector of the economy, but I still must ask: what happens when the money runs out? This type of policy clearly serves labor unions and small business involved in the sector, but the solution is very short-sighted in nature. What are we left with besides more efficient homes, massive debts and a bloated government? Energy conservation can only postpone the day of reckoning, when we have to face the fact we need more energy-generating capacity.

The moderator of the green conference commented, "If we don't do this now, we will look back in 20 years with regret." I thought, if we do this now, we will look back in 20 years and say to ourselves, what the hell were we thinking? Perhaps it was a good thing for him that all the attendees were bureaucrats and unionized contractors. Such programs become reality because politicians are out to please everyone in their quest for votes. *When you try to please everyone, no one ends up happy.* Instead of telling us what we need to do for the long term, they do what we want in the short term, costing us dearly. Leaders are not only supposed to carry out the wishes of their constituents but also educate and advise them of the long-term consequences of such wishes. Then they should propose and sell us an effective long-term course of action. Politicians, in the case of the Green Jobs initiatives, are doing nothing more than manipulating the public with key words and catchy phrases. None of this initiative reveals any substantive new science or innovation.

The private sector can advertise conservation, and we can buy the caulk at Home Depot and call the contractors ourselves. Then we can add these expenses to the cost basis of our house, thus reducing capital gains upon sale. (According to the U.S. Census Department, the average American moves every five years.) This mechanism is already in the tax code, and there is no need to create more overpaid bureaucrat jobs to manage something so simple. We definitely don't need auditors from the government's Department of Energy Weatherization and Intergovernmental Program making sure we did a good job insulating our homes. The fact that we insulated our homes correctly will be reflected in our monthly energy bills. Almost all utilities and online banking facilities allow us to download our bills and financial statements into a computer spreadsheet, where we can analyze our utility usage history.

If we continue on this path of statistical stimulus, we will end up worse than we started.

The current stimulus program can be equated to building driveways versus building freeways. Building driveways is low risk; it uses concrete and creates temporary jobs, but the project yield is not enough to cover its cost. It's a very superficial way of appeasing families in a time of need, but it does nothing for the collective good. On the other hand, we can mass all the workers and building materials for one large collective project, to build a freeway between two disconnected cities. This project is high risk, with more moving parts and potential obstacles; however, once complete, the resulting increase in commerce between the two cities will, over time, recoup the initial investment. This principle has been the basis for infrastructure development since the beginning of urban civilization.

In essence, our current stimulus efforts are just a patchwork mosaic, fixing potholes and appeasing special interest groups. We will hobble along until Santa Claus gives us money or Jesus forgives our debt. Government's role is to take collections of money and do what we individual Americans and private companies can't do: create big, capital-intensive projects that will in turn solve a myriad of other problems downstream, creating new opportunities and real economic demand.

Stimulating Fundamentals

Organic Stimulus is about creating an economic locomotive, an engine that pulls the rest of economy along. It creates demand based on fundamentals: population and wage growth, innovation, expanding production and developing exports. It does not mean borrowing money and spending it, only to find that the bill for the expired goods is greater than the original purchase price. This is in essence what the 2009 "cash for clunkers" program was about: encouraging people to borrow money for a car, which at the end of its life has no value. Meanwhile, the buyer has paid the purchase amount plus interest.

Organic Stimulus

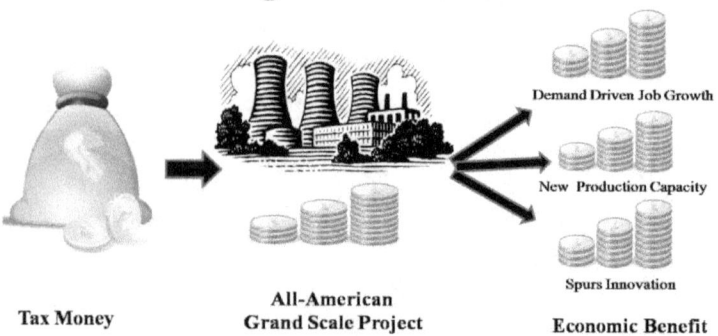

Organic Stimulus is taking a collection of money from the citizens and investing it into projects that yield greater and continuous returns downstream through economic enablement.

Organic Stimulus is about bringing money in from outside the boundary conditions (our borders) to expand the economy, thus expanding demand. This leads to a reduction in inventories, which stimulates business to expand capacity to keep up with demand. Businesses will not expand with tax credits alone; once the credit expires, the costs will remain. Elasticity exists where companies can hire temporary workers or utilize existing capacity by adding overtime to meet temporary spikes in demand. Stretching capacity is very good for the owners of the factories, who can get more out of existing resources. This may explain why we're not seeing much more hiring, despite all current stimulus measures.

Organic Stimulus is about thinking big and long-term, using debt for grand-scale projects that not only return the original amount invested but also spur growth in other sectors, which stimulates the overall economy for the long term. Governments are the ultimate investment banks, able to raise huge amounts of cash to fund game-changing projects. In essence, it is about the government doing what only government can do

Organic Stimulus is about government being able to recognize a public health crisis and intervene directly to protect our wellbeing, just as they did with quarantines and vaccinations during the tuberculosis and polio outbreaks in the early 20th century. Government must counterbalance against the large corporations that lose sight of the end consumer.

Organic Stimulus is vision and leadership, along with risk-taking based on lessons learned from history. This philosophy is clearly American and will enable many hardworking, bold and spirited people to become rich by providing goods and services that help build a nation. This philosophy calls for Americans to go back to the basics. Our country was built by entrepreneurs under the guidance of a strong government.

Organic Stimulus is also about our participation in all levels of politics. We need to elect leaders, not politicians. Currently, millions of dollars are being spent to show us where the billions are being wasted! And this needs to change. [90]

Organic stimulus not only creates immediate jobs, but also infrastructure and new technologies that create jobs in the future; these jobs more than compensate for the loss of the initial construction jobs. The gains in economic growth from these new projects pay back the borrowed money long term. Organic stimulus is also policy that enables growth and innovation, reducing barriers to small business and allowing immigration. We must bear in mind that GDP = GDP/Capita x Capita. To grow the economy, we not only need rising productivity (GDP per Capita) but also a rise in capita as well. Immigration not only grows the economy through natural demand for housing, consumer goods, etc but also by the fact diversity adds value and leads to innovation.

[90] Stephan Dinan, Millions go to signs flagging stimulus projects, *The Washington Times*, September 17, 2009

The Person to Person Bailout Plan

I first began thinking about the P2P Bailout Plan while I was living in Estonia, where Pier-To-Pier networking originated (i.e. Skype and Kazaa). My inspiration was the American Homestead Act, which was enacted into law by Abraham Lincoln in 1862. This Act gave an applicant a freehold title to up to 160 acres of undeveloped land outside of the original thirteen colonies. The new law required three steps: file an application, improve the land, and file for deed of title. In order to be eligible, one had to be the head of a family, at least 21 years of age, a citizen (or expecting to become one), and someone who never took arms against the Union. Those serving in the military were allowed to waive some restrictions. Conditions were liberal enough to encourage not only migration but also immigration from European countries. Eventually 1.6 million homesteads were granted totaling 270,000,000 acres. This came to 420,000 square miles privatized between 1862 and 1986 (Alaska allowed homesteading until 1986); this comprised a total of ten percent of all land in the United States. People were granted their share of the American Dream in exchange for making contributions to the economy. The Great Plains and Midwest, where most of this homesteading took place, are now among the most productive agricultural regions in the world.

In 2009, a total of 861,664 families lost their homes to foreclosure[91]. The government has spent $75 billion in

---

[91] Les Christie, Foreclosures up a record 81% in 2008, *CNN Money*, January 15, 2009

2009 to stem foreclosures; $700 billion through the TARP program was spent to back up banks with mortgages that are in default or in danger of defaulting.[92] Since the bailouts, we continue to see foreclosures at alarmingly high levels. According to RealtyTrac, in January 2010 the American foreclosure filings rose 15% from 2009 and exceeded 300,000 for the 11th consecutive month, as modification programs failed to keep delinquent borrowers in their homes.

The problem is that there is no real demand for homes. In real-estate agent classes, they teach that housing prices are determined mostly by the quality of the local job market, and by scarcity. In the current situation, we have neither jobs nor scarcity, as property was overbuilt in recent years. In order for housing to pick up, there must be demand from buyers who have reliable incomes. If we keep giving banks money to give to people without jobs, we are just going to keep banging our heads into the wall.

As an American working for a European investment bank, I met many people financially able to live in America, but who were discouraged by our current immigration laws. It inspired me to write the Person to Person (P2P) bailout program, a win-win situation for the American people and those from abroad wanting to live here.

The current program for an investor visa is quite limited in its ability to boost the economy, cumbersome in terms of processing and only available to a very few privileged people. The EB-5 Visa is an immigrant visa for an

---

[92] Congressional Budget Office, ABC News

investor and his family. A prospective immigrant must invest $1 million in a place of his choosing and create at least 10 new jobs. This program is limited to only 3,000 visas per year. The P2P bailout program is based on the EB-5 but is much broader and more simplified.

The Person to Person Bailout Program would in principle allow individuals from any visa-waiver country to obtain permanent residence (green card) in exchange for purchasing a home. The program would have the following provisions:

First: The buyer or immigrant must be from a country that is already in the U.S. Visa Waiver Program. These countries are: Andorra, Australia, Austria, Belgium, Brunei, Czech Republic, Denmark, Estonia, Finland, France, Germany, Hungary, Iceland, Ireland, Italy, Japan, Korea, Latvia, Liechtenstein, Lithuania, Luxembourg, Monaco, Netherlands, New Zealand, Norway, Portugal, San Marino, Singapore, Slovakia, Slovenia, Spain, Sweden, Switzerland and the United Kingdom. This measure will streamline the immigration process, as the above nations already have data sharing and security procedures in place which are in accordance with the U.S. Department of Homeland Security requirements.

Second: The buyer/immigrant(s) must purchase a home or condominium unit (with the intent to occupy) which is at least 10% above the median home price for the given area in the respective Metropolitan Statistical Area (MSA), using OFHEO data (Office for Federal Housing Enterprise Oversight) as a guideline. They must also follow local occupancy laws; a family of 10, for example, cannot move into a studio apartment. There will be a three-to-five year residency requirement for the given property, to avert speculation. The green card will only be awarded once this requirement has been met and verified.

Third: The prospective immigrant can finance no more than 70% of the home's value. The buyers/immigrants must demonstrate sufficient sources of income not only to pay their mortgage but also to support any family members who may accompany them. This income can be in the form of adequate pension income, state support to which they are entitled while living abroad, or sufficient personal resources such as dividend income, inheritance, personal wealth, family trust funds, etc.

Mortgage companies will have to qualify to be able to lend in this program. I propose that the mortgage payment can be no more than 25% of the buyers' gross income. The existing established relationships with the governments of visa waiver countries will also make it easier to implement procedures to verify income and assets.

These measures will ensure that new arrivals are investing a meaningful amount of money into our economy and that lender risks are minimized. The immigrants will help Americans who are having trouble selling their homes and will stimulate the economy with "imported" money. When they arrive, they will not only buy the home but they will also consume in the local economy. This program will eliminate costly ineffective government measures that are not working.

Hypothetically: the median price of a U.S. home is around $250,000, and there are over 500 million people living in the Visa Waiver countries. If just 1 million homes were sold through this program per year at $275,000 (10%

above the median) it would bring $275 billion into our economy per year, eliminating the need for the $700B TARP program altogether. Considering that the payment for such a home, assuming 30% down at a 6% mortgage rate, is around $1,155; the immigrant would have to be earning around $4,600 per month in gross income Assuming he conservatively pays 30% in taxes, both foreign and domestic, he has $2,065 per month in disposable income. With the strong euro and yen, there are many throughout Europe and Japan receiving generous corporate and state pensions who would easily qualify. Assuming one million annual participants, this puts around another $25 billion annually into the economy. If these immigrants start working, they will contribute even more to the overall U.S. economy. Best of all, this is money from abroad, which will help close existing trade imbalances.

Opponents of this plan argue that the immigrants may pose a security threat or inflate our population. But most of the population will be from European or Japanese origin. Additionally, one million over the current population of 308 million would increase our population by only 0.3%. We must also remember that immigration has led to our nation's greatest innovations: Google, Sun Microsystems, Cisco, and Yahoo, to name a few.

I sent this proposal to my Congressmen, the White House and some leading economists, but I received only form letters in return.

The Hydrogen Economy

In order for America to continue on a prosperous trajectory, it must achieve absolute energy independence. In addition to security risks, importing our energy contributes significantly to our trade deficit.[93]

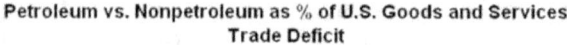

Petroleum vs. Nonpetroleum as % of U.S. Goods and Services Trade Deficit

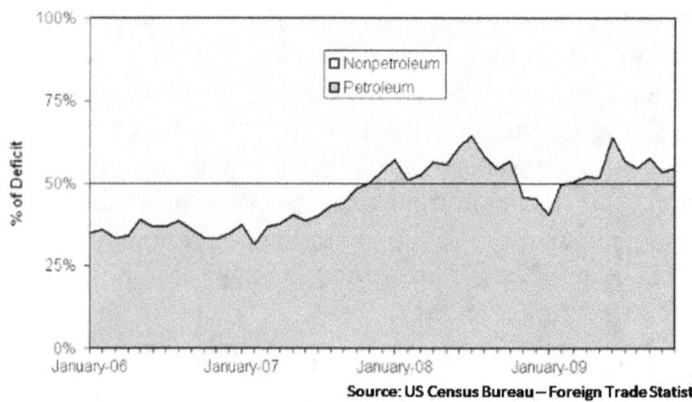

Source: US Census Bureau – Foreign Trade Statistics

According to Warren Buffet, "The U.S trade deficit is a bigger threat to the domestic economy than either the federal budget deficit or consumer debt and could lead to political turmoil... Right now, the rest of the world owns $3 trillion more of us than we own of them."[94] This imbalance results in the foreign countries that we trade with receiving more dollars than we receive of their currency (yen, euro, franc etc) in return. Thus the value of

---

[93] US Census Bureau: Foreign Trade Statistics – US Imports of Petroleum

[94] Associated Press, January 20, 2006

the dollar goes down over the long term, resulting in higher prices for imported goods. In everyday terms, this means that we will pay more for gas at the expense of movie tickets and other extras, compromising our standard of living. Moreover, the higher oil prices mean greater profits and a higher standard of living for nations like Iran, Venezuela, and Saudi Arabia.

Energy independence must be our nation's number one priority. Dependence on foreign energy sources is a clear and present danger to the integrity of our nation. This concept of eliminating this dependence is nothing new; it has been referred to as a "Manhattan Project" for energy.[95] However, it is political suicide for anyone in public office to initiate sweeping change. Currently, politicians are striving for energy independence by offering people tax credits for insulating their homes and buying hybrid cars. What we need is leadership that will force us to swallow this big pill that in the end will cure us of our petroleum-dependence cancer, which is slowly eroding the U.S. economy.

The Hydrogen Economy is built on the basic scientific principle that combining hydrogen and oxygen, with water as the only major byproduct, yields enough energy to do meaningful work. Hydrogen is very unstable, but fuel cell technology has resolved this issue and made the technology a viable alternative. Honda, Mercedes Benz, BMW, Hyundai and GM are all committed to bringing

---

[95] Lt. Col. John M. Amidon, America's strategic imperative: a "Manhattan Project" for energy, *Joint Forces Quarterly*, August 31, 2005.

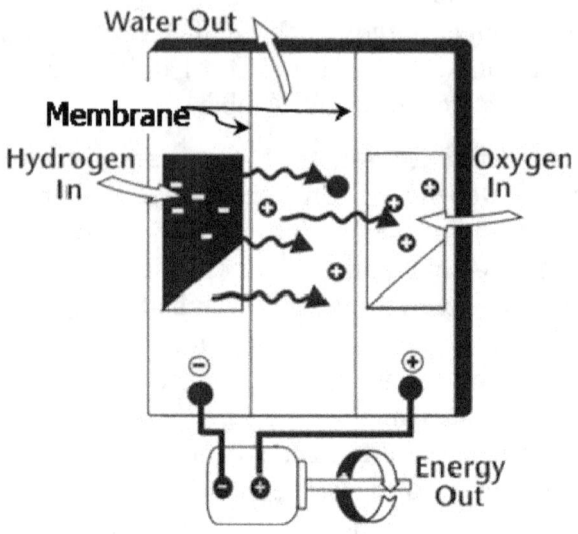

A common depiction of a fuel cell (Source: Wikipedia)

fuel cell vehicles to the market. Honda has already rolled out the FCX Clarity, a fully functional hydrogen-powered vehicle, in Southern California. BMW has introduced small quantities of its 7 Series, which runs on both hydrogen and petrol.

There are several obstacles to the mass distribution of these cars, such as cost and cold weather performance. A hydrogen fuel cell vehicle is estimated to cost at least $300,000. Much of this has to do with the limited quantities and infancy of the technology. Like any new technology, with adequate investment into large scale production, the costs should fall. Many experts and

178

automotive companies believe that one day that hydrogen fuel will be able to compete head on with petrol.[96]

The hydrogen fuel itself is derived from hydrolysis, running electric current through water. This separates the water into its basic components, hydrogen and oxygen, and requires a tremendous amount of electricity. Critics argue that this process will create more greenhouse gases than they save downstream. But that is only if we use fossil fuel based energy to generate the needed electricity. If the power were derived from nuclear, wind or solar, then there would truly be zero emission. Of these options, nuclear power is the most viable large scale solution to generating enough electricity to make enough hydrogen fuel for the U.S. economy.

Nuclear Energy is Essential

Nuclear power is making a comeback, despite its stigma. Even Patrick Moore, the co-founder of Greenpeace, agrees that nuclear power is the only viable large scale alternative energy sources that can vastly reduce greenhouse emissions while helping our nation achieve energy independence.

He writes in a Washington Post article[97]:

The 600-plus coal-fired plants emit ca. 2 billion tons of Carbon Dioxide annually -- the equivalent of the exhaust from about 300 million automobiles. In addition, the

---

[96] Robert Rose, Fuel Cell Q&A, *Breakthrough Technologies Institute* June 24, 2004

[97] Patrick Moore, Going Nuclear: A Green Case Makes Sense, *The Washington Post*, April 16, 2006

Clean Air Council reports that coal plants are responsible for 64 percent of sulfur dioxide emissions, 26 percent of nitrous oxides and 33 percent of mercury emissions. These pollutants are eroding the health of our environment, producing acid rain, smog, respiratory illness and mercury contamination. Meanwhile, the 103 nuclear plants operating in the United States effectively avoid the release of 700 million tons of CO2emissions annually -- the equivalent of the exhaust from more than 100 million automobiles. Imagine if the ratio of coal to nuclear were reversed so that only 20 percent of our electricity was generated from coal and 60 percent from nuclear. This would go a long way toward cleaning the air and reducing greenhouse gas emissions. Every responsible environmentalist should support a move in that direction.

New technologies, which include standardized designs with gravity-based safety mechanisms, make modern nuclear power an alternative that we must actively pursue, not only for our national security interests but also to meet the demands of future prosperity. In fact, there are over 436 nuclear plants worldwide, with China and S. Korea leading the way on new construction. While the U.S. has the most nuclear power plants (104), France derives 75% of its energy from the atom, the most of any nation. All of these plants, which span 32 countries with over 14,000 cumulative operating years, have run safely since the incidents at Chernobyl (1986) and Three Mile Island (TMI) (1979), the only two major reactor accidents in the history of civil nuclear power. TMI was contained without harm to anyone, and Chernobyl involved an intense fire without provision for containment. The designs of Chernobyl have been phased out and the last of these types of plants are in the process of being shut down. Thus the risks from Western nuclear power plants, in terms of the consequences of an accident or terrorist attack, are minimal compared to other commonly accepted risks.[98] In addition to creating clean energy, the excess heat (which, contrary to popular belief, is not radioactive) can be used for desalinization and water purification.

The barrier to investment for Nuclear Power Plants, like other infrastructure projects, is the upfront cost. However, much of this is due to regulatory bureaucracy and mismanagement. The plants that were built in the U.S. in the post-WWII era were all one-of-a-kind designs, with only a few plants similarly constructed. Thus, lack of standardization created additional regulatory and construction costs, making nuclear power in the U.S. an investment fiasco. The French were successful with their nuclear program because almost all of their reactors had the same design and procedures, allowing for easy interchange of parts and staff. Moreover, nuclear power plant construction in the U.S. was fragmented, completed by many different groups and consortiums, with no unified master plan.

The Westinghouse AP-1000 is an American-designed, standardized, advanced passive safety plant. It generates 1154 MWe and uses the forces of nature and relative simplicity of design to enhance safety and operations

---

[98] World Nuclear Association, Safety of Nuclear Power Reactors, March 2010

while reducing construction costs. According to Westinghouse, the AP-1000 design can be constructed in 36 months, from the pouring of first concrete to the loading of fuel. The simplified design includes water over the top of the pressure vessel so that gravity pushes water instead of pumps in the unlikely event of an emergency.

Improvements over previous generation reactors include:

- 50% fewer safety-related valves
- 80% less safety-related piping
- 85% less control cable
- 35% fewer pumps
- 45% less seismic building volume

Fewer parts mean fewer problems and reduced regulatory costs. The AP-1000 is the only Generation III+ reactor to receive design certification from the U.S. Nuclear Regulatory Commission (NRC). The Chinese already ordered four AP-1000 reactors and the first one is under construction. Moreover, five U.S. utilities have selected this design for future construction.

Waste Management

Any discussion of nuclear power inevitably raises the legitimate question of how to manage the waste. Nuclear fuel is quite compact to begin with: 1 kg of enriched uranium used for power generation corresponds to nearly 10,000 kg of oil or 14,000 kg of coal which enables the generation of 45,000 kWh of electricity. Spent nuclear fuel can be re-processed at a rate of up to 96%. This means that for every 100kg of spent nuclear fuel brought into a reprocessing facility, 96kg can be sent back out to the power plants to be used once again. Moreover, this process is repeatable. France's (Areva Company) has been doing this since the mid 1960s.

The 4% of unrecyclable waste that is left is plutonium, which in itself can be used for nuclear fuel; the remaining waste is incorporated into a glass matrix, trapping the radioactivity and preventing it from spreading, and then placed into stainless steel containers. The proven chemical stability of this borosilicate glass, used to immobilize the fission products, is in accordance with international standards regarding long-term integrity. This solidification guarantees water tightness and stability for hundreds of thousands of years.

These materials from spent fuel assemblies are compacted, their volume reduced to a fifth of their size. The end result is that the treatment of one ton of spent fuel generates less than 14 cubic feet of final residue, about the size of a typical refrigerator. All the nuclear waste in the last 40+ years in France would not even cover a football field if stacked 1 meter (3.3 feet high)! This solution is not perfect in the eyes of some groups, as we still do get some toxic and radioactive by-product. However, spent nuclear fuels reprocessing and waste management have remained proven disposal methods in France and Japan for more than two generations.

Yucca Mountain Nevada was proposed as America's high-level nuclear waste repository over a generation ago. It is a series of tunnels and caverns 1200 feet under Yucca Mountain. Although there was a two decade DOE study to confirm the integrity of this facility, opposition claims that in the next 10,000 years, the nuclear waste could be carried out by the water. However, the opposition never included vitrification (the transforming of radioactive waste into glassy substance which remains in a stable state suitable for long-term storage) assumptions in their studies. The opposition generally assumes that waste would be placed into containers as-is, which overtime would rupture, while water that seeped into the caverns over thousands of years would carry out the contamination into the general water supply, finding its way into the crops. Bear in mind that by the time this happens, the radioactive material would have mostly decayed away and become inert as well. The danger is not in the water's being exposed to radiation, but in its carrying particles that emit radiation (contamination). Hence, if the waste were vitrified, it would be a solid mass of glass that would remain intact for eons, even it were to come in contact with water (meaning that no contamination and thus no radioactivity would be carried downstream).

However, due to unprecedented bi-partisan cooperation by Democratic Senator Harry Reid and Republican Governor Jim Gibbons, the Yucca Mountain project was killed. The DOE withdrew its application without possibility of reversal in March 2010.[99] In fact, both Democrats and Republicans in Nevada built their campaigns around ending this project. No one ever stepped up to educate the public on how this solution, based on the French technology and in use since 1966, is

---

[99] Nicole E. Matthews, DOE Withdraws Application For Yucca Nuke Dump, *Fox News*, March 3, 2010

both sound and potentially profitable for the people of Nevada. The state could have built an economy on receiving waste from other states, reprocessing the nuclear fuel, and remanufacturing it back into fuel rods. The remaining waste would be placed deep into the caverns of Yucca Mountain (the cost of which would have been paid by the senders). In essence, Nevada could have been the new Alaska (which issues its residents an annual oil check).

Nuclear power is better than burning coal, the only other large scale energy source. In fact, the fly ash emitted by a coal plant—a byproduct from burning coal for electricity—carries into the surrounding atmosphere 100 times more radiation than a nuclear power plant producing the same amount of energy.[100] This is in addition to the greenhouse gasses and other pollutants that are not even present in nuclear power plants. Moreover, the mining of coal is extremely toxic to the environment, polluting rivers and water supplies. My former boss in Estonia told me, "The good thing about nuclear power is that you have 10,000 years to figure out what to with the waste, whereas with burning coal, it's an immediate problem."

Once such plants are built, the ongoing costs are quite competitive. There have been vast improvements in cost since the 1970s. Nuclear power operating costs are now at ca. 1.85 cents/kwh, whereas natural gas plants operate at

---

[100] Mara Hvistendahl, Strange but True, *Scientific American*, December 13, 2007

around 4.06 cents/kwh and oil-fired plants operate at 4.41 cents/kwh (2002)[101].

Hence, the source for American-generated emission-free electricity required to enable the hydrogen economy is already in place. It just needs to be pushed through the highest levels of government. Nuclear power in and of itself is not a viable private sector business; it is more of an economic enabler to energize other sectors of the economy that could not exist without such infrastructure in the first place. Spinoff benefits from giant infrastructure are realized over the long term.

DOD/DOE Management Partnership

In addition to the French, the U.S. Navy has been an exceptional manager of nuclear reactor and power generation technology. The Navy states that during more than 60 years of operating nuclear power plants at sea, it has never had an accident. The U.S. Navy has standardized the designs, created a training pipeline and a system of checks and balances to make sure that the highest standards are met. Ship-and-submarine-based reactors are far more complicated than terrestrial-based civilian ones; thus, the Navy is the ideal manager for the nation's power generation capacity.

Already there are military bases (Army, Navy, Air Force, and Marine Corp) throughout the country that may double as sites for our new nuclear power plants. The land is already federally owned and secure.

---

[101] Nuclear Energy Institute, Nuclear Power Plants Maintain Lowest Production Cost for Baseload Electricity, September 3, 2003

Energy is of strategic importance to our nation's security, making it logical that the military should take charge of power generation. I believe that they would certainly do it more cheaply than the private sector. Navy Nuclear officers and enlisted men can be rotated from sea duty to civilian nuclear duty, which in many cases would be close to their homes, as military bases are dispersed all over the nation. This may help retention in the Navy Nuclear community and perhaps even attract more recruits who might see this as a viable career path. Also, upper management will be executives paid at the Commander and Captain level, with a few executives paid at the Admiral level; this is a far cheaper management structure than in the private sector at places like Dominion Power

This DOE/DOD partnership approach will streamline nuclear power and make it competitive with conventional sources of energy. The Navy Nuke logic will help reinforce the idea of standardized design and quality management to ensure the process is running at maximum efficiency. We are in dire times and must optimize all of our resources. Congress needs to push for such a merger that allows a profitable civilian–military partnership that ultimately benefits the American taxpayer/consumer.

The Smart Grid and BPL

Electrical grid and transmission infrastructure will parallel the building of the new nuclear power plants and the hydrogen economy infrastructure. Already, the current stimulus allocates only $3 billion for the smart grid, which is only to rebuild existing electrical infrastructure and install some thermostats and energy management software. If we were to do this on a grand scale, we could rebuild our entire electrical infrastructure so that it cannot only deliver electricity but also deliver the internet to everyone who has access to electricity, especially those in remote regions.

Broadband over Power Lines (BPL) is already running in places like Manassas, Virginia. Many of the limitations have to do with the fact that internet signals can be run within local regions only up to the transformers, those yards that you see filled with electrical equipment throughout the community. However, new smart grid transformers could allow for the transmission of internet, which could fundamentally change our nation. According to the FCC, about 93 million Americans (35%) don't have access to high speed internet. This is mostly due to the cost of the service, which averages $41 per month.[102]

Not only can BPL deliver internet through an existing power outlet, but it can also deliver it much more cheaply, since it works within some of the existing and proposed electrical infrastructure.[103] The current stimulus for smart-grid and new-grid infrastructure projects will call for the installation of the transformers that can handle BPL. There are still some issues being worked out with radio frequency interference, but I believe the right investment into technology can solve this.

If the poor can gain access to information, then they gain access to education and market options. They may be able

---

[102] John B Horrigan PHD, Broadband Adoption and Use in America, *FCC*, February 2010

[103] Motorola, Practical, Proven Broadband over Power Line, February 2006

to take courses online, learn about the effects of compounding interest on payday loans, shop for used books and also find household items at much lower cost. Access to knowledge almost always leads to good things. When I was at Sears in 2001, a coworker and I envisioned a data delivery network for the service technicians, in which they could use high-speed internet to download the latest manuals and training materials to stay current in their job, paying a fixed cost instead of per-minute dial-up costs.

Such an information superhighway would boost the effectiveness of our workforce all over our country, which would lead to productivity gains and ultimately a wealthier nation.   The amazing fact is that BPL implementation can be piggybacked onto the new electrical grid infrastructure at marginal cost while creating an economic enabler.

Big Projects, not Big Government

The greatest dilemma facing the Hydrogen Economy is the chicken or egg conundrum. It can't be introduced on a large scale unless there are enough hydrogen-powered cars. The hydrogen powered cars can't be bought unless the infrastructure exists to fuel them.[104] This technology is 20 to 50 years off. However, I am sure that with a deliberate and unified effort we can push this along much faster. If we managed to go from vacuum tubes to transistors to the first silicon microchips in the span of a

---

[104] Geoff Cunningham Jr., Hydrogen dilemma, *The Mercury News*, March 5, 2010

generation, surely with all our current technology, we can push the Hydrogen Economy to the forefront as well.

Shifting our energy dependence from petroleum to hydrogen will be no easy task, and it is one that only a government can to take on. Government is not meant to distribute caulk, windows and insulation. Instead, its role is to undertake strategic projects too expensive for the private sector. Such government projects (like building highways, bridges and dams) lay the groundwork that enables private sector economic growth. There is nothing wrong with borrowing and spending massive amounts of money if it will pay off in the future

Economic Locomotives

The following are examples of grand-scale projects from the past that enabled today's $14 trillion economy. These projects gave rise to new industries never imagined before their completion.

The First Transcontinental Railroad

The First Transcontinental Railroad was built by the Central Pacific Railroad of California and the Union Pacific Railroad between 1863 and 1869. It connected its statutory Eastern terminus at Omaha, Nebraska with the Pacific Ocean at Alameda, California, on the eastern shore of San Francisco Bay. By linking with the existing railway network of the Eastern United States, it connected the Atlantic and Pacific coasts of the United States by rail for the first time.

The discovery of gold in California in 1849 sent people racing to inhabit and exploit the state. Suddenly, plans for a Transcontinental Railroad that only several years earlier were ridiculed as over-ambitious were revived, resulting in an 1853 act of Congress, authorizing the construction of the railroad. However, conflicting interests between North and South prevented an agreement from being reached on the route.

Ironically, it was not until the outbreak of the Civil War that the Transcontinental Railroad became a reality. With Southern opposition removed from positions in federal government as a result of secession, the Senate and House of Representatives seized on the opportunity and passed the Pacific Railroad Acts in 1862 and 1864, which eventually paved the way for the construction of the railroad. The Congress supported it with 30-year U.S. government bonds and extensive land grants. Opened for through traffic on May 10, 1869, with the driving of the "Last Spike" at Promontory Summit, Utah, the line established a mechanized transcontinental transportation network that revolutionized the population and economy of the American West.

The transcontinental railroad is considered one of the greatest American technological feats of the 19th century. It served as a vital link for trade, commerce and travel that joined the eastern and western halves of late 19th-century United States. The railroad quickly ended most of the far slower and more hazardous stagecoach lines and wagon trains that preceded it. The railroads led to the decline of traffic on the Oregon and California Trails which had populated much of the west. They provided faster, safer and cheaper transport for people and goods across half a continent. A trip would take 8 days and cost $65 in economy class.

The sales of land-grant lots and the transport of timber and crops led to the rapid settling of the American interior. The main workers on the Union Pacific were Army veterans and Irish immigrants. Most of the engineers and supervisors were Army veterans who learned the railway business during the Civil War. The Central Pacific, facing a labor shortage in the West, relied on Chinese immigrant laborers.

Needing rapid communication, the rail companies built telegraph lines along the railroad rights of way as the track was laid. The linkage made these lines easier to protect and maintain than the original First Transcontinental Telegraph lines, which went over much of the original routes of the Mormon Trail and the Central Nevada Route through central Utah and Nevada. They soon superseded the earlier lines, which were mostly abandoned.[105]

The Panama Canal

The Panama Canal was one of the largest and most difficult engineering projects ever undertaken; the 48-mile long canal had an enormous impact on shipping between the Atlantic and Pacific oceans, replacing the long and treacherous route via Cape Horn at the southernmost tip of South America. A ship sailing from New York to San Francisco via the canal travels 6,000 miles, well under half the 14,000 miles route around Cape Horn. Annual traffic has risen from about 1,000 ships in the canal's early days to 14,702 vessels in 2008.

The concept behind the canal dates to the early 16th century. The first attempt to construct a canal in that same location was in 1880 under French leadership. But the project was abandoned after 21,900 workers died from malaria and yellow fever from treacherous tropical weather. The United States launched the second effort while Panama was under Columbia's rule. After much debate over which route to pursue, the Hay-Herran Treaty was signed On January 22, 1903, which in turn was ratified by the United States Senate on March 14, 1903. However the Columbian Senate did not ratify the treaty. Philippe Bunau-Varilla, chief engineer of the French canal company, told Roosevelt and Hay of a possible

---

[105] Wikipedia- The First Transcontinental Railway

revolt and hoped that the U.S. would support them with troops and money.

Theodore Roosevelt changed tactics, promising support for Panama's intermittent separatist movement. On November 2, 1903 U.S. warships blocked sea lanes against Colombian troops who were coming to put down the revolt, while dense jungles blocked land routes. Panama achieved independence on November 3, 1903 when the United States sent naval forces to encourage Colombia's cooperation in this matter. The United States quickly recognized the newly independent Panama. Also in November 6, 1903, Phillipe Bunau-Varilla, Panama's ambassador to the United States, signed the Hay-Bunau Varilla Treaty, granting rights to the United States to build and indefinitely administer the Panama Canal. The blockade was cost effective and served a distinct purpose—it isolated Columbia, then offering a diplomatic and monetary solution, avoiding a long drawn out quagmire that would have drained our finances and ultimately our war fighting ability.

The United States, under President Theodore Roosevelt, purchased rights to the French equipment and excavations for $40 million and began work on May 4, 1904. The United States paid Colombia $25 million in 1921; seven years after completion of the canal, for redress of President Roosevelt's controversial role in the creation of Panama. Colombia recognized Panama under the terms of the Thomson-Urrutia Treaty.

John Frank Stevens, Chief Engineer from 1905 to 1907, argued against a sea-level canal (like the French had tried to build) and convinced Theodore Roosevelt of the necessity of a system of locks and dams. Stevens' primary

194

achievement in Panama was building the infrastructure necessary to complete the canal. He rebuilt the Panama Railway and devised a system for disposing of soil from the excavations. He also built housing for canal workers and oversaw investment in extensive sanitation and mosquito-control programs that eliminated disease from the area — particularly malaria and yellow fever, the source of which had been identified as the mosquito by Cuban physician and scientist Dr. Carlos Finlay in 1881. Finlay's theory and investigative work had recently been confirmed by Dr. Walter Reed, while in Cuba with the U.S. Army during the Spanish-American War. Hence, the canal project led to innovations in medicine as well.

Construction of an elevated canal with locks finally began in earnest. The Americans gradually replaced the old French equipment with machinery designed for a larger scale of work, like giant hydraulic crushers. President Roosevelt had the former French machinery minted into medals for the workers to commemorate their contributions.

In 1907 Roosevelt appointed George Washington Goethals Chief Engineer of the Panama Canal. The building of the canal was completed in 1914, two years ahead of the scheduled completion date of June 1, 1916. The canal was formally opened on August 15, 1914, with the passage of the cargo ship SS Ancon. Coincidentally, this was also the same month that World War I began in Europe. While advances in hygiene had resulted in relatively low casualties during construction, 5,609 workers did die during the period from 1904 to 1914. This brought the total death toll for the construction of the canal to around 27,500; the final cost was $352 million, which in today's dollars would be ca. $7.9 billion.[106]

The U.S. controlled the canal and the surrounding area until 1977. The Torrijos–Carter Treaties provided for the transition of control to Panama. From 1979 to 1999 the canal was under joint U.S.-Panamanian administration, and in December of 1999, command of the waterway was assumed by the Panama Canal Authority, an agency of the Panamanian government.[107]

The Hoover Dam

The Hoover Dam, in the Black Canyon of the Colorado River between Arizona and Nevada, is one of the most impressive feats of engineering in American History. When completed in 1936, it was both the world's largest hydroelectric power generating station and the world's largest concrete structure. It still remains one of the world's largest hydroelectric generating stations.

In 1922 a commission was formed to build the Dam. The federal representative was Herbert Hoover, then Secretary of Commerce under President Warren Harding. In January 1922, Hoover met with the state governors of Arizona, California, Colorado, Nevada, New Mexico, Utah, and Wyoming to work out an equitable arrangement for apportioning the waters of the Colorado River for their states' use. The resulting Colorado River Compact, signed on November 24, 1922, split the river basin into upper

---

[106] CNBC, Big Budget Events Slideshow:
http://www.cnbc.com/id/27717424/Big_Budget_Events?slide=1

[107] Wikipedia: The Panama Canal

and lower halves with the states within each region deciding how the water would be divided. This agreement, known as the Hoover Compromise, paved the way for the project. The intended purpose of this project was to provide irrigation, flood control and hydroelectric-power.

The first attempt to gain Congressional approval for construction of Boulder Dam, the original name, came in 1922 with the introduction of two bills in the House of Representatives and the Senate. The bills were introduced by Congressman Phil D. Swing and Senator Hiram W. Johnson and were known as the Swing-Johnson bills. The bills failed to come up for a vote and were subsequently reintroduced several times. In December 1928, both the House and the Senate finally approved the bill and sent it to the President for approval.

On December 21, 1928, President Calvin Coolidge signed the bill approving the Boulder Canyon Project. The initial appropriation for construction was made in July 1930, by which time Herbert Hoover had become President. While approval took only six years in an age of handwritten and telephone communication, we have been waiting almost two generations to gain approval for a grand-scale nuclear power project.

Construction began in 1931, under the direction of Six Companies, Inc. This was a joint venture of Morrison-Knudsen Company of Boise, Idaho; Utah Construction Company of Ogden, Utah; Pacific Bridge Company of Portland, Oregon; Henry J. Kaiser & W. A. Bechtel Company of Oakland, California; MacDonald & Kahn Ltd. of Los Angeles; and the J.F. Shea Company of Portland, Oregon. The chief executive of Six Companies,

Frank Crowe, had previously invented many of the techniques used to build the dam. Much of the scientific and construction techniques had to be developed along the way. During the concrete-pouring and curing portion of construction, for example, it was necessary to circulate refrigerated water through tubes in the concrete. This removed the heat generated by the chemical reactions that solidified the concrete. The setting and curing of the concrete was calculated to take about 125 years without mechanical cooling. Six Companies Inc. discovered that such a large refrigeration project was beyond its expertise, and they hired the Union Carbide Corporation to assist with the refrigeration needs. Hoover Dam was completed in 1936, a little more than two years ahead of schedule! The dam and the power plant are now operated by the Bureau of Reclamation within the U.S. Department of the Interior.

Although this project was an unprecedented feat in public and private sector cooperation, it had problems as well. Officially, 96 men lost their lives during construction, but another 42 would die later, due to health complications attributed to the working conditions.

Today Hoover Dam produces power at around 5-6 cents per kilowatt hour which includes the cost of building the dam capitalized over its lifetime [108] which is almost half the average cost of residential electricity of around 11-12 centers per kWh.

---

[108] Wikipedia: Hoover Dam

The Interstate Highway System

The Dwight D. Eisenhower Federal System of Interstate and Defense Highways, commonly called the Interstate Highway System, is a network of freeways and expressways named for President Dwight D. Eisenhower, who championed its formation. The entire system as of 2006 was 46,876 miles in total length, making it both the largest highway system in the world and the largest public works project in history. The Interstate Highway System is a subsystem of the National Highway System. While Interstate Highways usually receives substantial federal funding (90% federal and 10% state) and complies with federal standards, they are owned, built, and operated by the states or toll authorities, and provide an excellent example of how states and federal governments can work together.

The freeway system serves nearly all major U.S. cities, with many Interstates passing through downtown areas. The distribution of virtually all goods and services involves "The Eisenhower" at some point. Residents of American cities commonly use urban Interstates to travel to their places of work. The vast majority of long-distance travel, whether for vacation or business, uses the national road network; of these trips, about one-third of the total number of miles driven in the USA in 2003 was driven on the Interstate System.

The Interstate Highway System was authorized by the National Interstate and Defense Highways Act of 1956, on June 29 of that same year. It had been lobbied for by major U.S. automobile manufacturers and championed by President Dwight D. Eisenhower, who was influenced by his experiences as a young Army officer crossing the country in 1919 on the Lincoln Highway, the first road across America. As Supreme Commander of the Allied forces in Europe during World War II, Eisenhower also gained an appreciation for the German Autobahn network as a vital component of a national defense system. In addition to facilitating private and commercial transportation, it would provide key ground transport routes for military supplies and troop deployments in case of an emergency or foreign invasion. Eisenhower was a true visionary general, understanding of how the economy and national defense are intertwined. He was able to align military needs with the economic needs of the nation. The DOE and DOD merger to generate domestic power aligns the strategic defense need for energy independence with upgraded and increased power generation infrastructure required for future economic expansion.

Although construction on the Interstate Highway System continues, I-70 through Glenwood Canyon (completed in 1992) is often cited as the completion point of the originally planned system. The initial cost estimate for the system was $25 billion over 12 years; it ended up costing $114 billion (adjusted for inflation, $425 billion in 2006 dollars) and took 35 years to complete. Interestingly enough, as the highway system grew, the economy also grew, creating demand for more highways.

Additional spurs, loops and bypasses remain under construction, such as Interstate 485 in North Carolina, under construction since 1988. A few main routes not part of the original plan remain under construction as well, like Interstate 22 in Tennessee, Mississippi, and Alabama, and the extension of Interstate 69 from Indiana to Texas.

Officials have also identified some non-Interstate corridors for future inclusion into the system.

There was no way to predict the long-term economic benefits when this plan was conceived. New unforeseen industries were born out of the freeway system, just as new industries were born out of the internet. As a result, new cities were built, advances in logistics were made and a new tourism industry emerged..[109]

Land of Dreams

America must remain the land where the impossible becomes possible. I am not sure how we lost our way. But if we are ever to even maintain what we have, let alone advance, we need leaders willing to take risks and willing to convince us of delayed gratification. Our nation's identity has been defined by thinkers like Thomas Jefferson, Howard Hughes, Ben Franklin, and Willis Carrier. We need some more people like them.

---

[109] Wikipedia: Eisenhower Freeway System

Solving the American Food Crisis

Food Expenses as a Percent of Household Income, 2007

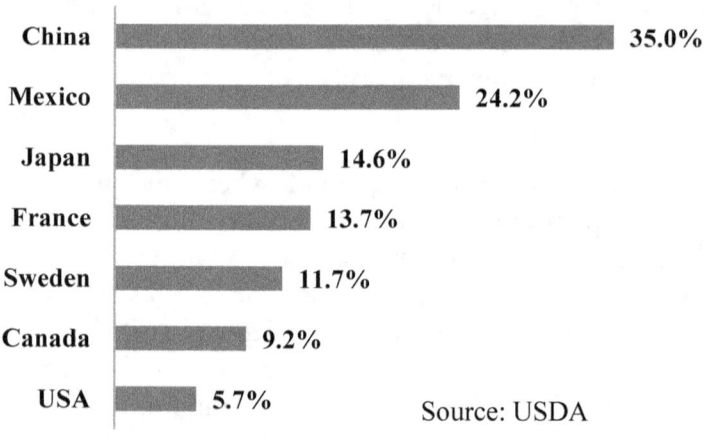

China — 35.0%
Mexico — 24.2%
Japan — 14.6%
France — 13.7%
Sweden — 11.7%
Canada — 9.2%
USA — 5.7%

Source: USDA

Much of our nation's success can be attributed to our ability to produce massive amounts of food very cheaply. In fact, we are better at food production than any other nation on earth. American agriculture has spurred innovations in engineering, genetics, logistics and economics. In the early days, states set up Agriculture and Mechanical and land grant schools where farmers could learn new techniques and share practices to boost crop yields. Meanwhile, massive investments made in rail, highways, and canals increased efficiency in the movement of food to the marketplace, resulting in even lower food prices. Consequently, we enjoy a standard of living never seen before in the history of the planet.

US Obesity Rate
Percentage of Population - Source: OECD

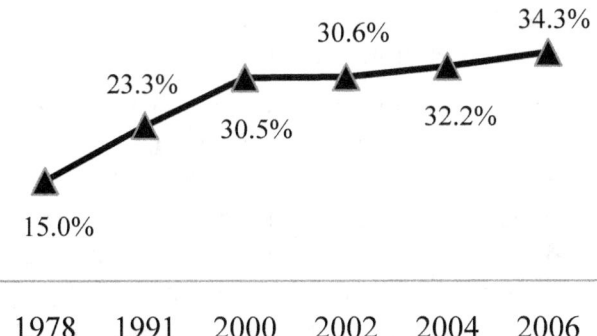

| 1978 | 1991 | 2000 | 2002 | 2004 | 2006 |

Cheap food has given us greater disposable income, which has enabled our uniquely American consumer economy. The demand for consumer products continues to drive innovation, most notably in the automotive, electronics and consumables sectors. Perhaps it also led to innovations in leisure and entertainment as well. With the power of massive disposable income, we are able to enjoy movies like Avatar and go to places like Disney World. In essence, innovation and engineering in basic needs industries has led to demand for innovation in other sectors, like science and business.

However, the same innovation that gave us such a high standard of living is now playing a large role in our undoing. Our food crisis is not one of food shortage but one of overabundance. We are becoming a fat nation, plagued with health problems like cancer, heart disease, diabetes and depression. This is already costing U.S.

companies $45B[110] per year and the U.S. Economy $100B per year[111] in medical expenses and lost productivity due to absenteeism. Obesity and related illnesses are associated with a 36% increase in spending on healthcare services, more than smoking or drinking.

When my wife and I returned to America we realized just how much we are being bombarded with food marketing advertising along with being a time-impoverished society. Career demands do not leave much time for exercise to counteract all this rich food, and walking is not a part of everyday life as it is in Estonia and Europe My evening walk home in Estonia was not only exercise but also an excellent "decompression" time.

Healthcare = Health + Care

Our nation needs to overhaul the current system for medical care. Our life expectancy is not rising in accordance with what we are spending on healthcare. But we have to fix our health before we can offer care.

We consistently wait to fix problems after they appear, rather than fixing them before they happen at lower cost; we fix only what is visible. We need to invest in preventative measures first before we can undertake a universal care system that is financially feasible over the

---

[110] Linda Barrington & Barbara Rosen, Weights & Measures: What Employers Should Know about Obesity — Key Findings, *The Conference Board*, May 2008

[111] Martha Mendoza, AP: Nutrition Education Ineffective, *USA Today*, July 4, 2007

long haul. Americans in their current collective physical state will surely rupture any nationalized health care plan.

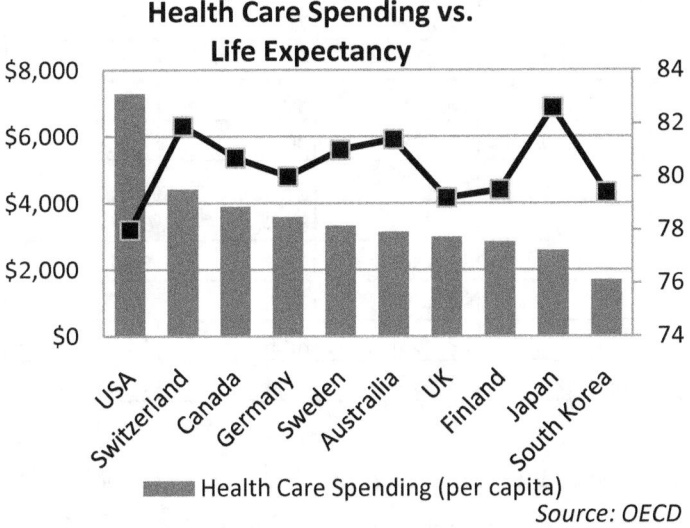

Health Care Spending vs. Life Expectancy

Health Care Spending (per capita)

Source: OECD

Fixing the health part is going to be much harder than fixing the care part. It will require a lot more than running one big bill through Congress. Recalibration of the food processing and medical industries, as well as readjustment to our work environment, will have to be undertaken. However, this pro-active preventative approach will cost less and be far more effective than a reactive system but we will have to redesign the way we live.

Country	Health Care Spending (per capita)	Life Expectancy	Annual Doctor Visits
USA	$7,290	78	3.8
Switzerland	$4,417	81.9	4.0
Canada	$3,895	80.7	5.8
Germany	$3,588	80	7.5
Sweden	$3,323	81	2.8
Australia	$3,137	81.4	6.1
UK	$2,986	79.2	5.1
Finland	$2,840	79.5	4.2
Japan	$2,581	82.6	13.6
South Korea	$1,688	79.4	11.8
			Source: OECD

Americans spend the most and get the least from healthcare.

This is a tough battle to fight when the U.S. food industry spends $10B per year in clever marketing campaigns, mostly aimed at children, to promote fast food, soft drinks and sugared cereals. These are high margin items that lack proper nutrition. The average child sees and hears around 10,000 food advertisements per year, most of which are for junk food. Marketing campaigns link fast food and soft drinks to toys, movies and celebrities. In contrast, the entire federal budget for nutrition education is around $1B per year.[112]   Soft-drink companies have established lucrative contracts with cash-strapped school districts

---

[112] Martha Mendoza, Nutrition education ineffective, *AP*, July 4, 2007

tying financial incentives to sales![113]   This is tragic, considering that childhood obesity rates are at an all-time high, up 500% among 6-11 year olds and up 300% among 2-5 year olds since the 1970s, according to CDC data.

Country	Life Expectancy	Overweight & Obese (%)	Smoking Rate (%)	Beef Consumption kg/capita
USA	78	67.3	15.4	40.2
UK	79.2	61	21	17.3
Australia	81.4	58.4	16.6	35.1
Germany	80	49.6	23.2	16.8
Finland	79.5	48.9	20.6	16.8
Canada	80.7	46.8	18.4	32.3
Sweden	81	44	14.5	20.2
S. Korea	79.4	30.5	25.3	12.3
Switzerland	81.9	27.3	20.4	21.3
Japan	82.6	25.1	25.7	9.4
				Source: OECD

Life Expectancy, Obesity, Smoking and Beef Consumption: Smoking is not the only culprit affecting life expectancy; we need to examine other factors as well.

Smoking is no longer the major factor of concern among children and teens. For a very long time we have focused on eradicating smoking from our society, but we have done very little to address the excessive high-calorie, low nutritional-value foods and beverages. The focus of our health care overhaul needs to be on creating regulations

---

[113] Kelly D. Brownell and David S. Ludwig, Fighting Obesity And the Food Lobby, *The Washington Post*, June 9, 2002

and safeguards that address the root causes of obesity. This approach will in turn make a universal health care system affordable, as less people will be demanding treatment. This will make a public health care program feasible.

Solving the root causes of obesity may also resolve other issues that plague our society such as depression, loneliness and low self-esteem. Moreover, addressing the obesity issue is a matter of our national pride and identity. Good looks are rooted in healthy behaviors. Athletic and fit people naturally look better than people who sit on the sofa during their free time. There was a time back in the 1950s when average Americans, not just the movie stars, were considered the best looking people all over the world.

Roots of Obesity

Everyone is on a diet, but we are still fat. People are reading the labels and counting calories, but they continue to struggle with their weight.

I believe that our biggest problem is our consumption of red meat and soda, including diet soda. Per capita soft drink consumption in children has grown five-fold since 1954, and soft drinks are now the most consumed beverage of kids 10 and older. Soda pop in general contains high amounts of caffeine and phosphoric acid which may impede the absorption and metabolism of calcium by the body. Given that few American kids consume adequate amounts of calcium to begin with, these kids are at risk in the future for osteoporosis.[114]

Soda-Pop Consumption
(Gallons per Year)

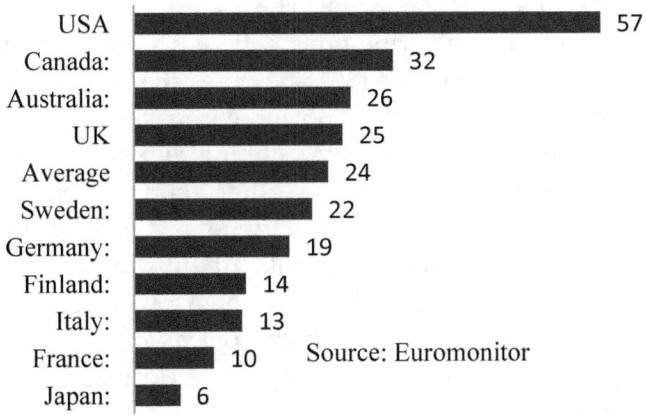

Country	Gallons
USA	57
Canada:	32
Australia:	26
UK	25
Average	24
Sweden:	22
Germany:	19
Finland:	14
Italy:	13
France:	10
Japan:	6

Source: Euromonitor

No one in the world drinks soda the way we do. The Weston A. Price Foundation refers to this as "America's Other Drinking Problem.". Each gallon contains almost 1600 calories!

The controversial ingredient in soft drinks is the sugar or high fructose corn syrup. There is really no difference between sugar and corn syrup; they both deliver the same amounts of fructose. People have been consuming sugar for well over 2,000 years. There is nothing wrong with the

---

[114] Food and Drink Weekly, Per capita soft drink consumption up 500% over last 50 years, May 10, 2004.

substance itself; it is the quantities that we consume that are dangerous.

Drinking diet soda is not any better. According to a study by Sharon P. Fowler, MPH, and her colleagues at the University of Texas Health Science Center, San Antonio, the risk of becoming overweight is in fact greater with diet sodas than regular ones! The findings show that for each can of diet soft drink consumed each day, a person's risk of obesity went up 41%. She notes that diet sodas do not cause obesity, but they do increase risk of becoming obese. People believe that by drinking diet soda they can allocate the saved calories to other foods, namely fast food. Leslie Bonci, MPH, RD, who is the Director of Sports Nutrition at the University of Pittsburgh Medical Center, states that diet drinks by themselves are not the root of America's obesity problem, but if you are on a diet and your only change is a switch to diet drinks, you will not lose weight. [115]

Thus it appears that soft drinks may need to be regulated in the same manner as alcoholic ones. Consuming excessive amounts of soft drinks may not get us drunk, but the long-term effects may be just as detrimental as hard drinks, especially in children. Each year, Americans consume an additional 33 gallons of soda-pop over normal Western consumption levels, amounting to 52,800 extra calories or an additional 15 pounds per person per year (1600 calories per gallon of cola and 3,500 calories per pound). A 155-pound man would have to run 75

---

[115] Daniel J. DeNoon, Drink More Diet Soda, Gain More Weight?, *WebMD Health News*, June 13, 2005

miles per year at a 10 minute-per-mile pace, which amounts to 13 hours, just to offset this excess amount – a lot of extra work.

The easiest way to get society to choose water or milk over soft drinks is to subject soft drinks to sin taxes in the same manner as alcohol and tobacco products; we also need to set a drinking age for soft drinks so that we can protect children from targeted marketing.

Moreover, if Americans could reduce their average beef consumption of 86 pounds per year to European levels of 37 pounds per year, they would reduce their intake by 68,629 calories annually, or 20 pounds per capita (hamburger meat contains 1,386 calories per pound, and one pound of fat contains 3500 calories) Our excess consumption above western norms would require a 155 lb. man to run 97 miles per year at a 10 minute per mile pace, amounting to 16 hours, just to offset this excess intake. Once again – a lot of extra work. In essence, our excess consumption of hamburger and pop is giving us an extra 35 pounds per year to contend with.

Reducing our consumption of red meat will solve other problems as well. It takes 8kg of grain[116] and 3,682 liters (approximately 1,000 gallons) of water[117] to make 1 kilogram (2.2 lbs) of beef. Thus, a reduction in our consumption to normal levels would save 53,000 square

---

[116] UN Food and Agricultural Organization

[117] J. L. Beckett and J. W. Oltjen, Estimation of the Water Requirement for Beef Production in the United States, Department of Animal Science, University of California, Davis, 1993

miles of land- roughly the area of Arkansas. Moreover, we would save 6.7 trillion gallons (6 cubic miles) of water, or 21,000 gallons per American, about half the water consumed annually per person. It would also reduce our nation's overall water consumption by 5% (based on Organization for Economic Co-operation and Development data), not to mention the energy associated with moving all this fluid around. Water in and of itself is becoming a scarce commodity, and we must be cautious of its overuse.

The general state of uneasiness in our country is causing stress and lack of sleep. Calorie intake and exercise by far affect our weight the most. However, recent studies at the University of Bristol in the UK (also replicated in the USA) show that stress and lack of sleep also contribute significantly to weight gain. The body needs down time to recover and recharge. Studies indicate that sleep-deprived people crave more sweets and starchy food as well. Sleep is essential to our health.[118]

Who is Driving the Train?

One has to ask who is standing between us and good health policy. The titans of the food and beverage industry are highly educated and intelligent people, and they should be ensuring that society can continue on a sustainable path.:

- Warren Buffet is a major shareholder of Coca Cola and one of the world's richest men. Despite the fact he

---

[118] BBC News, Obesity Linked To Lack Of Sleep, December 7, 2004

is a frugal billionaire, we don't see him advocating for regulations on child consumption of soft drinks.

- Indra Nooyi, originally from India, is the CEO of PepsiCo and considered one of the most powerful women in the world. Her 2009 compensation was $14.2 million. We don't see her using this power to improve the health of children.

- Irene Rosenfeld, a mother of two and Cornell PhD, is the CEO of Kraft Foods. She picked up $26.3 million in compensation in 2009, up 41% from 2008. I wonder if she feeds her kids macaroni and cheese every day.

These people can afford to do the right thing. They are in a position to start applying logic and common sense to the greater good without fear of consequence. They can advocate balanced-life policies for their employees, which ensure that employees get exercise and family time so that their productivity can be sustained.

Why don't these people step up and start making changes for the greater good?

The Doctor's Role:

Since tribal times we have revered our medicine men. Throughout history, doctors have been influential in shaping public affairs.

It is believed that our medical system is the greatest in the world. But if this is true, why are we experiencing such a problem with obesity? The answer is that our medical system is great at emergencies–after-the-fact care. No one has better trauma surgeons and specialists than we do. But we are not very good at before-the-fact care.

Becoming an American doctor is like becoming a professional athlete; it is a very selective and rigorous process requiring both natural intellectual gifts and a self-disciplined, determined work ethic. Moreover, it's a very expensive process; students spend well over $100,000 on their education.

Perhaps doctors should step up as a group. They are among the most highly educated people in our country, earnings at the top of the American workplace spectrum. The American MD commands more respect than any other professional. I could never understand why as a group they haven't stood up to the food and beverage companies by creating a Political Action Committee (PAC), pushing for legislation that regulates soda pop and beef.

Doctors are complacent. But if we are healthier as a whole, the doctors and drug companies will collectively lose business. The good news is that we only need a few active doctors in each district. If debt relief was offered to doctors advocating for a healthier food and beverage industry, it might help change our nation. Such doctors will emerge as community and industry leaders.

Perhaps we are taking short-cuts at the expense of our health because we want such cheap food? But deciding to live healthier lives will help save our planet and increase our quality of life and happiness. Good health requires an investment of our time and a shift in our mindset, which is not easy at first, but the rewards are sustainable and everlasting.

PART IV – REALITY

Compounding Debt

Debt to GDP: Past and Present: Many argue that our national debt is not so bad today, that we had higher Debt to GDP levels during and after WWII.

US Debt to GDP Ratio (%)

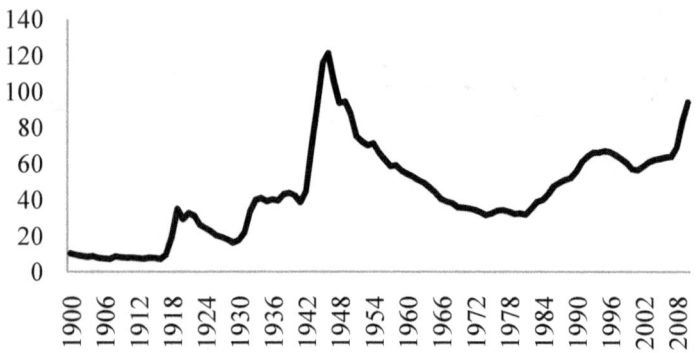

Many also argue that war is good for the economy. After all, the end of WWII brought a postwar economic boom and baby boom, which brought about a powerful American middle class consumer economy that was the envy of the world.

However there is a difference between borrowing back then and borrowing today. Back in those "good-old" days, debts were a result of building infrastructure— public works projects such as the highways, dams and airports, enabling future economic growth. Today we are borrowing to give tax breaks, fill some potholes and pay for some windows, none of which enables future economic growth. These expenses only maintain what we have. Tax money needs to be invested, not just spent, if we are ever to improve our standard of living and quality of life.

I personally believe that tax breaks are mostly bad; we end up paying more. Taxes are a collective of public funds to get bulk buying power, much like taking a collection from office colleagues and then buying your coffee in bulk from Sam's Club instead of individually going to 7-11 and paying 3x as much on a per-cup basis. It is better to pay taxes and spend the money on economic enabler projects, which will not only create more jobs but also lower overall costs down the line, much like the railway did for travel across the interior of the country. Spending tax money on Hoover Dam created cheap electricity, which enabled the Southwest, namely Las Vegas, to grow. It's either save a buck today and take the tax break or save a couple of quarters every year for the rest of your life. We are in a sense paying for these tax breaks through lower quality education in our public schools, crumbling roads and bridges and overall inflation in the cost of living. Somewhere sacrifices have to be made, or our lack of education and poor infrastructure will severely hinder our future ability to grow.

World War II grew the U.S. economy because much of the war expense was invested into new steel mills, airplane and tank factories and shipyards, all of which were also used by the private sector after the war. This infrastructure enabled the postwar economy to surge, as America became an industrial powerhouse. Today, much of the war expenditure is being spent on rebuilding Iraq and Afghanistan, which has no meaningful future returns for the U.S. economy. Many of the materials used to build Iraq and Afghanistan also do not originate from America, and therefore do nothing for our economy. The War on Terror does not invest into the future of the American economy. Instead we are hiring a lot of government workers who don't add additional value; in the past, we hired government workers to create infrastructure.

It is similar to the difference between a hired concrete worker and a hired security guard. They may cost the same, but one has no tangible return. We used to write checks to ourselves, but now we write checks to others with no hope of being repaid.

|Absolute Value Matters|

In absolute terms, our current debt levels are very high at $13 trillion, while our economy's ability to keep up is questionable.

In the past, our absolute debt was only a few billion dollars during a period of expansion, and did not put our country at risk. Moreover, in the past we borrowed from ourselves and from friendly nations. Now as the absolute value of debt takes off, along with the interest it accrues, we put ourselves at the mercy of foreign nations. We have to bear in mind, this interest accrues whether we are spending, investing or sitting on the money while we do studies on how best to spend it. Hence, the longer we wait and the less decisive we are, the more expensive the debt becomes.

US GDP vs. Debt
Absolute Terms ($ billions)

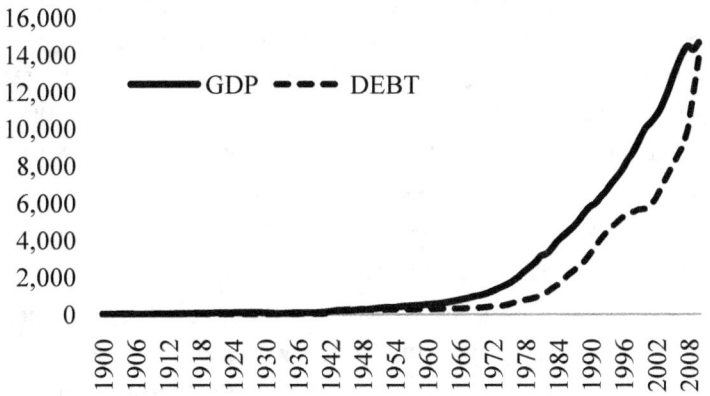

Debt is surging while GDP growth is stalled

In essence: before, we were like college graduates who borrowed money to build a cupcake factory during a period of economic expansion. Now we are the middle-aged adults who borrow to pay for imported cars and ADT security systems, while the economy sinks.

The recent jump in debt was not due to investment spending, which returns something in the future, but was mainly due to expenses. The current stimulus that patches roads and completes small projects will only get us back to the status quo, not advance our economy. If we are to advance, it either needs to pay-off this debt or increase GDP at a faster rate; otherwise we can expect something unexpected and without warning.

2.77 Hours per Day

Nothing happens unless we as individuals make it so. Living in a democracy demands more of its citizens. The more we participate as individuals, the better the system works. The more we leave greater amounts of decisions to fewer elected officials, the less it works – for us. We spend on average 2.77 hours per day watching TV (2008), according to Bureau of Labor Statistics, even as we are complaining that we have no time. It seems we have lost control of our lives, becoming slaves to corporations and servants to those we elected.

The business model for politicians is much like a fitness center that profits by signing up more members than they actually can support. Gyms see a surge in memberships around New Years, but most of the new sign-ups stop showing up after a month. The gym caters to the needs of its core group of regulars, while the no-shows pay for most of the costs.

We must remember that every time we make a choice, we are in effect voting. We can use our dollars and how we spend our money to draw the attention of the corporate leaders. When we start attending local town hall or neighborhood civic league meetings, we will start to notice that those we elect will actually start listening to us. The more we participate as everyday citizens, the more they will listen. Participating in a democracy need not be a full-time job. We only need to participate more often with greater consistency

We need to demand better qualifications for those we elect. We need to demand that our leaders at all levels are highly knowledgeable about economics, finance science, and basic math. Math has this pervasive habit of always being right, absolute and unemotional. Leaders need to understand the nature of math. They need to understand the uses of information technology, be inquisitive, and most importantly know and understand the history of the United States of America.

We are living in an age where it's cool to be stupid. We see the media glamorizing people who act silly, get DUIs, shoplift, or cheat on their wives. Collective stupidity has cost us dearly. America has abundant the natural resources, strong infrastructure and good core government policies, but there is a problem in the control box. Success is all about management at the top. If we look at Russia, we see that this country has more land, oil, timber and PhD's than any other nation, yet they are still lagging behind many nations in economic development. Japan, on the other hand, has very little natural and land resources. But they are wealthier than Russia because of better top level management. Russia's largest barrier is a belligerent and aggressive mentality, which is also becoming our major impeding factor to progress. Electing cheerleaders, frat boys and pro-wrestlers may be cool and fun, but in reality it is harmful

Brains and academics do matter. People in public office need the intellectual horsepower and education to deal with globalization and decoupling. They need to listen to us and to lead us. They need to stand up to us at times as well. Leaders must be able to always look for ways to make the public sector more efficient and ensure that our money is being spent on economic enablers and not on building bureaucracies. Leaders must have vision, but more importantly, they must have the ability to communicate this vision to us. When we start electing smart, educated and visionary people, we will get more out of our tax dollars and see the quality of public services increase.

Quantified Consciousness

On average, we earn $19.41 per hour, according to Bureau of Labor and Statistics If we took an hour out of our TV time to read about our government and its policies, we would be knowledgeable enough to write our political leaders and make a collective impact. We are a nation of do-it-yourselfers, and now it's time for DIY politics.

If the 231 million Americans over 18 (2008 US Census, American Community Survey) participated one hour per day in democracy, the macro effect would be the equivalent of $4.5B per day or $1.1 trillion per year in lobbying efforts (one hour per day/240 days per year). This would stomp out the efforts of the 13,739 lobbyists who spent a combined total of $3.5B in all of 2009 to promote their agendas.[119] Lobbyists would not make such investments in elected officials unless they reaped tangible and reliable returns. The amount invested and the number of lobbyists is growing every year, and it is about time we make sure those we elect and pay through our taxes are listening to us as well!

Perhaps if we could get off the sofa and see the world for ourselves, we may also get to know our families better, burn some calories, and learn a lot. Walking every

---

[119] Lobbying Database: www.opensecrets.org/lobby

weekday for an hour will burn 48,000 calories per year, which is 14 lbs. Perhaps some will pursue creative activities that lead to breakthrough innovations or cultural advances as well.

If we are to remain the America that innovates, creates, overcomes hardship and does the impossible, we have to push through the tiredness and exhaustion, stop watching other people's lives and invest time into our own. Remember, we are the country best known for inventing revolutions from our garages. Despite all the money and efforts of large corporations and special interest groups, we still retain the power of the vote. Stupidity and ignorance are expensive. We can no longer afford the luxury of ignorance. Politics affects of our lives as much as work, family and eating. It is no longer *cool to be stupid* about current affairs, geography and culture. But if we all start learning and start caring, we can turn these difficult times into an unprecedented period of innovation.

It's ultimately up to us.

DIY Resources

Democracy works best when we all take part. First, get involved locally, where the changes will be the most visible; then work your way up. Eventually the collective efforts of acting locally will start to make a national impact. Write often and demand answers that are not put in form letters. Be sure to vote at every single opportunity; it is so important.

Civic Leagues: Your neighborhood may have a civic league which advocates for stop signs, speed bumps, building codes etc. They may also set up neighborhood watch groups.

Write Your US Congressional Representative:
They run for office every two years!
www.house.gov

Write Your Senator:
They run for office every six years!
www.senate.gov

Write the President of the United States
www.whitehouse.gov

Lobbying Activity:
See who is trying to seduce your congressional representatives. Click on "Top Spenders" and see if their interests really do match yours.
http://www.opensecrets.org/lobby/

Track Progress. See how salaries, employment, demographics and industry have changed in your location over time. www.USCensus.gov and www.bls.gov

Find Facts. Learn about agriculture, medicine and government finance. www.usda.gov, www.cdc.gov, www.gpoaccess.gov/usbudget

Website and Social Media:
We aim to create an interactive community where we can share resources on how to discover information for ourselves:

www.TheOrganicStimulusPlan.com

Facebook: The Organic Stimulus Plan

The Beginning....